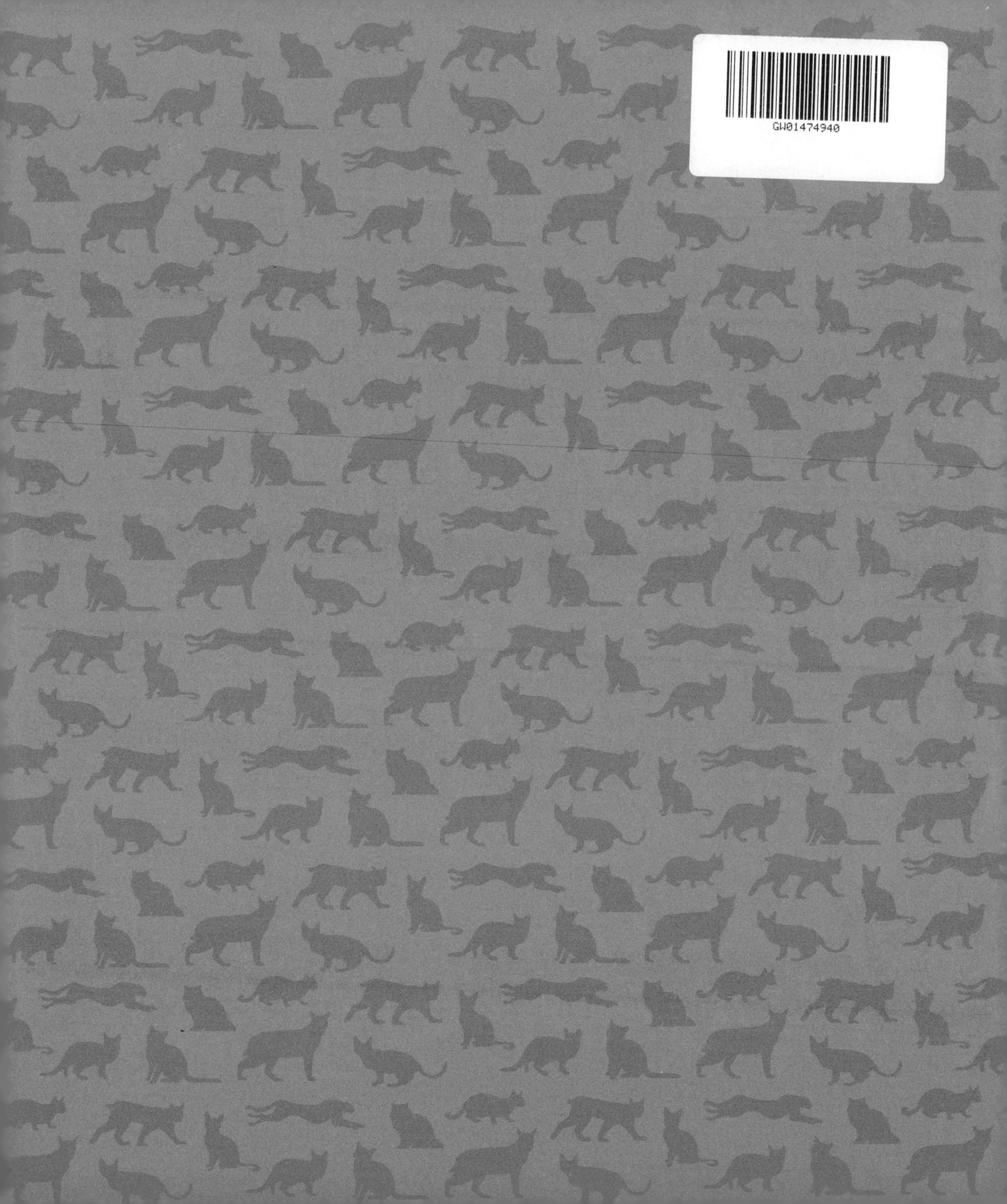

ATLAS of CATS

For five special feline friends – Charlie, Arthur, Beau, Purrley and Cleo.
F. E.

To Hugo: tiny tail, big heart.
K. H.

Author: Frances Evans
Illustrator: Kelsey Heaton
Publishing Director: Piers Pickard
Publisher: Rebecca Hunt
Editorial Director: Joe Fullman
Art Director: Andy Mansfield
Commissioning Editor: Kate Baker
Designer: Kim Hankinson
Consultant: Camilla de la Bedoyere
Print Production: Nigel Longuet

Published in August 2024
by Lonely Planet Global Limited
CRN: 554153
ISBN: 978-1-83758-260-0
10 9 8 7 6 5 4 3 2 1

Printed in Malaysia

All rights reserved. No part of this publication may be reproduced, stored in a retrieval system or transmitted in any form by any means, electronic, mechanical, photocopying, recording or otherwise except brief extracts for the purpose of review, without the written permission of the publisher. Lonely Planet and the Lonely Planet logo are trademarks of Lonely Planet and are registered in the US Patent and Trademark Office and in other countries.

Although the author and Lonely Planet have taken all reasonable care in preparing this book, we make no warranty about the accuracy or completeness of its content and, to the maximum extent permitted, disclaim all liability from its use.

Stay in Touch
Lonelyplanet.com/contact

Lonely Planet Office:
IRELAND
Digital Depot, Roe Lane (off Thomas St), Digital Hub, Dublin 8, D08 TCV4, Ireland

Paper in this book is certified against the Forest Stewardship Council™ standards. FSC™ promotes environmentally responsible, socially beneficial and economically viable management of the world's forests.

Lonely Planet Kids

ATLAS
of
CATS

illustrated by
Kelsey Heaton

written by
Frances Evans

CONTENTS

- 6 A World of Cats
- 8 Atlas of a Cat
- 10 Super Senses

DOMESTIC CATS

- 12 Introduction
- 14 Longhaired and Shorthaired Cats

North America
- 16
- 18 Sphynx, Cymric, Tonkinese
- 20 Selkirk Rex, Somali, American Bobtail, Pixiebob
- 22 *Courageous Cats*
- 24 Maine Coon, Exotic Shorthair, Balinese
- 26 Ragdoll, Ragamuffin, Snowshoe
- 28 American Shorthair, American Wirehair, American Curl
- 30 LaPerm, Lykoi, Munchkin, Minuet
- 32 Bengal, Ocicat, Toyger
- 34 *Cat Shows*

Europe & Africa
- 36
- 38 British Shorthair, British Longhair
- 40 Persian, Scottish Fold, Manx
- 42 Cornish Rex, Devon Rex, Suffolk, Seychellois
- 44 *Cute Kittens*
- 46 Birman, Chartreux, Aphrodite
- 48 German Rex, European Shorthair, Norwegian Forest Cat
- 50 Egyptian Mau, Sokoke
- 52 *Cats in Ancient Egypt*

Western & Northern Asia
- 54
- 56 Russian Blue, Donskoy, Siberian, Kurilian Bobtail
- 58 Turkish Van, Turkish Angora, Turkish Shorthair
- 60 Kanaani, Arabian Mau
- 62 *How to Speak Cat*

Southern, Southeast and East Asia & Australasia
- 64
- 66 Li Hua, Singapura, Japanese Bobtail

68 Khao Manee, Korat, Siamese
70 Abyssinian, Mekong Bobtail, Ceylon, Burmese
72 *Oriental Cats*
74 *Asian Cats*
76 Australian Mist, Mandalay, Templecat
78 *Natural Instincts*

WILD CATS

80 Introduction

North & South America
84 Canada Lynx, Bobcat, Puma
86 Jaguar, Margay, Ocelot
88 Andean Cat, Geoffroy's Cat, Jaguarundi, Pampas Cat, Northern and Southern Tiger Cats, Kodkod
90 *Cat Culture*

Europe & Asia
94 Eurasian Lynx, Iberian Lynx, European Wildcat
96 Tiger, Snow Leopard, Pallas's Cat
98 Asiatic Wildcat, Chinese Mountain Cat, Jungle Cat, Rusty-spotted Cat, Fishing Cat, Leopard Cat
100 Flat-Headed Cat, Asiatic Golden Cat, Bay Cat, Clouded Leopard, Marbled Cat

Africa
104 African Lion, Leopard, Cheetah
106 Sand Cat, Serval, African Wildcat, Caracal, Black-footed Cat, African Golden Cat
108 *Record-breaking Cats!*

110 Glossary
112 Index

A WORLD OF CATS

Welcome to the wonderful world of cats! From the Siamese and the Siberian to the puma and the caracal, this book will take you on a claw-some journey around the planet to meet more than 60 domestic cat breeds and 40 species of wild cats. Some are kitties you might spot in your neighbourhood or species that you've seen on TV, while others will be less familiar felines.

WHAT IS A CAT?

Cats are meat-eating mammals, known for their agility, gracefulness and fierce hunting skills. Apart from Australia and Antarctica, cats are native to every continent on Earth.

All cats belong to the feline (or Felidae) family, which is split into two main groups: big cats and small cats. The big cats (or Pantherinae) include the lion, tiger, jaguar, snow leopard, leopard, clouded leopard and Sunda clouded leopard. The small cats (or Felinae) include other wild cat species and the domestic cat.

There are thought to be about 100 million wild cats in the world.

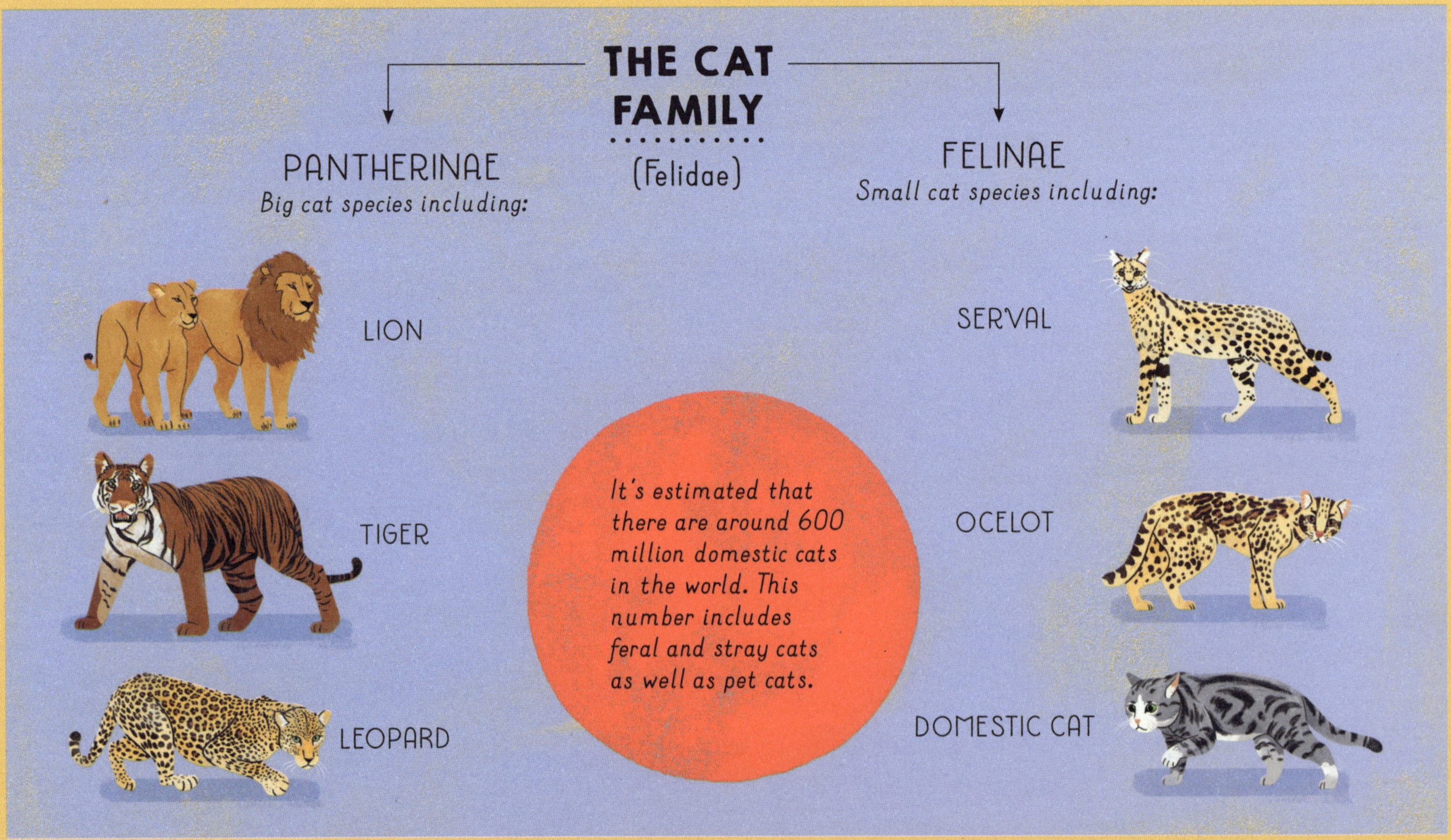

THE CAT FAMILY
(Felidae)

PANTHERINAE
Big cat species including:

- LION
- TIGER
- LEOPARD

FELINAE
Small cat species including:

- SERVAL
- OCELOT
- DOMESTIC CAT

It's estimated that there are around 600 million domestic cats in the world. This number includes feral and stray cats as well as pet cats.

CATS AND US

On the one hand, cats are deadly, powerful predators. On the other, they are some of our best-loved animal friends, bringing comfort and companionship to millions of people around the world. The fact that domestic cats are descended from such independent wild animals is part of what makes the bond between humans and cats so special. Ultimately, cats could get along just fine without people, but they often choose to share their lives with us.

Some domestic cats choose to live a wild life. They are known as 'feral cats'. Feral cats have usually had little or no contact with humans and behave more like wild animals than pets.

HOW THIS BOOK WORKS

This book is split into two halves. The first half introduces you to domestic cat breeds; the second half takes a deep dive into the world of wild cats.

You'll find a map at the start of each chapter, which shows you where each breed or wild cat species comes from. Each cat featured on the map has its own profile within the chapter. For the domestic cats, the profiles give you the lowdown on the breed's background and care needs. For the wild cats, the profiles explore each species' behaviour, habitat and conservation status.

Throughout the book, you will also find special entries that explore topics such as heroic cats, kittens, natural instincts and show cats.

CONSERVATION STATUS

For the conservation status, we have used the IUCN Red List of Threatened Species, which grades species from Least Concern to Near Threatened, Vulnerable, Endangered, Critically Endangered, Extinct in the Wild and Extinct.

ATLAS OF A CAT

Whether they're the king of the jungle or the queen of your sofa, all wild and domestic cats share the same essential features. Here's some basic cat geography.

BODY STRUCTURE

Cats' bodies are built for speed and agility. Long, powerful legs allow cats to run fast and pounce on prey. Their spines are incredibly flexible, thanks to extra-thick pads of elastic-like material between the bones, and strong muscles. If cats fall, their bendy backs mean they can twist themselves around in mid-air, so they (usually) always land on their feet.

TAIL

Most cats have long tails, which they use for balance when walking or climbing and to express how they're feeling. Some breeds of domestic cat, such as the American bobtail shown here, have a short tail. Others, such as the Manx, have no tail at all. Manx cats have strong back legs and an arched back to make up for their lack of a tail and help them balance.

COAT

Wild cats have short hair, but domestic cats have been bred to have short hair, long hair, curly hair or sometimes no hair at all. Some cats have a 'double coat', made up of a thick underlayer of hair and a rougher, outer layer. In the wild, a cat's coat keeps it warm and is important for camouflage, helping it to blend in with its surroundings and sneak up on prey.

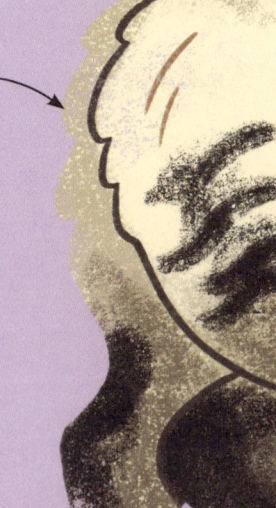

PAWS

A cat has a thick paw pad for each of its toes. These pads act as shock absorbers, protecting the cat's feet when it's walking or running. They also soften the sound of a cat's movement, allowing it to creep up on prey.

EAR SHAPES

Most cats have upright ears, with rounded or pointed tips. Some domestic cats have been bred to have unusual-shaped ears. For example, the Scottish fold has folded ears, while the American curl has ears that curl backwards.

TONGUE

If you're ever licked by a cat, you'll notice its tongue feels rough, a bit like sandpaper. Cats have tongues that are covered in tiny hooks called 'filiform papillae'. These hooks help the cat clean its fur and, in the wild, scrape every morsel of meat off a carcass.

WHISKERS

All cats have long, sensitive hairs, called whiskers, on their face. Whiskers help a cat feel its way around and make sense of its environment. Never trim your cat's whiskers – cutting a cat's whiskers is painful and makes the cat feel disorientated.

TEETH

An adult cat has 30 teeth in total. The four fang-like teeth at the front are called canines and they're used for stabbing prey. Cats can't chew like humans. They use the sharp teeth (called molars) at the side of their mouth to cut up meat and then swallow it.

Cats can open their mouth very wide and have strong muscles to give them a powerful bite.

Retracted claws

Extended claws

CLAWS

Cats have sharp claws to hunt and catch prey, and to help them climb. Just like your fingernails, a cat's claws are made from a strong material called keratin. Apart from the cheetah, all cats have claws that can be pulled back (or 'retracted') under special folds of skin when they're not using them. This prevents the claws getting broken or worn down and it also allows the cat to quietly creep up on prey.

SUPER SENSES

Like humans, cats rely on their senses – smell, sight, hearing, taste and touch – to explore the world around them. But the way cats use their senses is quite different to us. Let's take a look.

HEARING

While a person can hear someone talking from up to 150 metres (500 feet) away, a cat can hear the same sound from about 750 metres (2,500 feet) away – five times further than a human. Cats are also capable of detecting high-pitched noises (like squeaks) that are three times higher than what we humans can hear. Their pointed ears contain 32 muscles which allow them to swivel their ears 180 degrees to find sounds – a bit like furry satellite dishes.

SMELL

An average house cat has around 40 times more scent receptors in its nose than you. Its superior sniffing power helps it locate prey when it's hunting. Cats also use smell to communicate. Think about the way a cat greets you. When a cat rubs itself against your leg, it is transferring its scent and marking you as part of its gang. Transferring scent is also comforting for a cat – by rubbing its scent all over you, the cat is making you smell more familiar.

Cats have a second 'nose' in the roof of their mouth. It is called a 'vomeronasal organ' and it allows the cat to get information about other felines from special chemicals called pheromones, which are found in cats' wee.

Cats can see some colours, though not quite the range that we can. It's thought they can see blue and yellow colours best, while red and green shades appear grey to cats.

SIGHT

Cats are most active at dawn and dusk (known as being 'crepuscular') and their eyes are purpose-built for hunting in dim light. If you live with a cat, you might notice that its pupils are sometimes thin slits and sometimes wide circles. A cat's pupils naturally get wider at night to allow the cat's eye to take in as much light as possible and help it see in the dark. A cat's pupils get thinner in daylight or a brightly lit room because it doesn't need to let in as much light to see. Cats can also see a much wider area than we can, which helps them spot prey. They can't see very far, however, without things looking blurry.

TASTE

Taste is the only sense that is less than super in a cat. A pet cat only has around 470 taste buds compared to your 9,000. Although they are thought to be able to detect sour, bitter, salty and umami (savoury) flavours, cats can't taste sweet things.

TOUCH

Cats have touch receptors all over their bodies and are sensitive to touch, especially on their paws and nose. But their most important touch tools are their whiskers. Cats use their whiskers to navigate the world by brushing them against objects. They also use their whiskers to pick up vibrations in the air, helping the cat detect moving prey or approaching danger.

The next time you see a cat try to climb through a hole in a fence or squeeze through a tight space, take a look at what it does with its whiskers. Cats will put their head through openings first, using their whiskers like a ruler to measure whether they can make it through the gap.

Introduction to DOMESTIC CATS

From fluffy ragdolls and sleek Bengals to smooth sphynxes and marvellous moggies, there are thought to be over 200 million cats living in human homes around the world today. They all belong to the same species, *Felis catus* – also known as the domestic cat or house cat.

HOW CATS BECAME DOMESTICATED

It is thought that humans and cats have had a close relationship for at least 9,000 years. The ancestors of today's house cats were African wildcats (p106) that probably chose to start living near humans. Where there were humans, there were stores of grain, and where there was grain, there were mice for the cats to feed on. People saw how useful it was to have a live-in mouse catcher and encouraged the cats to stick around. Over time, these cats became tamed (or 'domesticated').

The ancient Egyptians (p52) are thought to be the first people to treat cats as pets. The special status of cats in ancient Egypt led to them being introduced, possibly as precious gifts, to Europe and Asia on trading ships. Later, when Europeans started sailing to the Americas and Australia, they took their feline friends with them, helping domestic cats to spread across the world.

WHAT IS A BREED?

A group of cats that have been deliberately bred to have the same characteristics is known as a 'breed'. Cats that are a mix of several breeds or have unknown ancestry are commonly known as 'moggies'.

Different breeds have been developed in different parts of the world, and they often reflect the environment they come from. The rugged Maine coon (1) was bred to keep New England farms free of mice, the nimble Sokoke (2) emerged from the forests of Kenya, and the easy-going Australian mist (3) was made for an indoor-only life in modern Australian cities.

Breeding cats so they have a particular look and personality is a fairly new thing. Some old breeds have been around for centuries, such as the Chartreux and Siamese. But most modern breeds have been developed in the last 150 years.

OWNING A CAT

Cats are wonderful companions, and welcoming one into your family is very exciting. But owning a cat is a big responsibility. A well-cared-for cat can live for 16 years or more, so it's important to think about how your lifestyle will suit a cat and how you will look after it throughout its life.

The best way to get a cat is to adopt through a rescue or rehoming centre, where all sorts of fabulous felines are cared for before being matched with loving homes. If you decide to buy a cat, make sure you use a reputable breeder who will be an expert on the breed and takes good care of their animals. Never buy a kitten online without seeing it with its mum in a happy home environment.

LONGHAIRED & SHORTHAIRED CATS

Whether they're a breed or a moggie, domestic cats can be split into two main groups – longhaired and shorthaired. When choosing a cat, the length of its coat and the amount of care it requires is an important thing to consider.

FABULOUS FLUFF

Longhaired cats have masses of soft hair, which can be ten times longer than the coats of shorthaired cats. These fluffsters make beautiful pets, but they need a lot of care and commitment from their owner to keep them that way. You will need to brush a longhaired cat every day to stop its coat from getting tangled or matted.

The ragdoll is a popular longhaired breed. Like many longhaired cats, ragdolls have laid-back, gentle natures.

The Siberian is an example of a longhaired breed whose coat originally had a practical purpose – keeping it cosy during freezing Russian winters.

Some longhaired breeds, such as the Persian, have a very dense double coat, which makes it hard for these cats to wash themselves properly – they rely on their owner to keep them clean and healthy.

SLEEK AND SHORT

Shorthaired cats can easily groom themselves and usually only need a weekly brush to keep them looking their best. Because they have lighter, streamlined coats, these cats are generally more active than their longhaired cousins.

Although sphynx cats look completely hairless, most have a very fine, delicate layer of fur covering their bodies. Their hairless appearance is caused by a genetic mutation.

The exotic shorthair was developed to have the same looks and character of the Persian but with a shorter, more easy-to-care-for coat.

The Cornish rex is an example of a shorthaired cat with a curly, or 'rex', coat. The curly hair is caused by a special gene.

FUR PHRASES

In the wild, the colour of a cat's coat has one job – it helps the cat to blend in with its surroundings and sneak up on prey. As a result, wild cats have quite a limited range of coat colours and patterns. In contrast, humans have deliberately bred domestic cats so they come in an incredible range of colours and patterns. Here are some useful fur-related words that you will find in this book.

Solid – a cat that is all one colour. Also known as 'self coloured'.

Bicolour – a cat that has a white coat with patches of one other colour.

Tricolour – a cat with a white, red (or ginger) and black coat. Also known as 'calico'.

Colourpoint – a cat with a pale-coloured body and darker markings on its paws, tail and face.

Tipped – a coat where only the tip of each hair is coloured. The rest of the hair is usually white or silver.

Ticked – a coat where each individual hair is striped. Also known as 'agouti'.

Tabby – a coat with a stripy pattern.

Tortoiseshell – a coat that's a mix of black and orange colours, often with brown and gold flecks.

DOMESTIC CATS · NORTH AMERICA

SPHYNX

The sphynx is actually a modern breed. Its origins lie not in ancient Egypt but in Ontario, Canada, where a hairless kitten called Prune was born in 1966. The sphynx is called a 'hairless' breed, but that's not entirely true. Although some have no hair whatsoever, most sphynx have a very soft, fine layer of downy fur. The sphynx's lack of a proper coat means it gets hot and cold very easily, so it should be kept as an indoor cat.

The breed's prune-like appearance isn't for everyone, but behind those wrinkles is an incredibly affectionate cat that wants to be as close to its favourite human as possible. A sphynx will delight in chasing feather toys or rattle balls and eagerly snuggle up under the duvet beside you at the end of the day. They make excellent therapy cats due to their sweet natures and love of a warm lap.

The ancient Aztecs are said to have bred hairless cats in the 1300s and 1400s.

- Wedge-shaped head
- Few or no whiskers
- Big ears
- Large, piercing eyes
- Sturdy body
- Slender neck
- Slim legs with neat, round paws
- Long, whip-like tail

CAT STATS
Country: Canada **Coat:** Usually has a very fine, thin fuzz of hair, but can be completely bald **Colours and patterns:** Various colours and patterns, including white, black and red, and tabby, tortoiseshell and tricolour **Personality:** Loving, outgoing, inquisitive

Hairless cats lack the gene that allows their fur to grow properly and have appeared naturally all over the world for centuries.

CYMRIC

If you're looking for a bobtail breed with a bit of floof, look no further than the Cymric. Confusingly, the name Cymric comes from Cymru, the indigenous name for Wales, despite the cat having no connection to the country. The breed was actually developed in Canada in the 1960s.

These roly-poly cats are a longhaired version of the more practical Manx (p41) and share all the characteristics of their short-coated cousin – they're good-natured, playful and excellent at jumping thanks to their long, powerful back legs. Cymrics are also particularly nimble with their paws and can even learn to open cupboards or doors!

CAT STATS
Country: Canada **Coat:** Long and glossy
Colours and patterns: All colours and patterns, including black, brown, chocolate, cinnamon, blue, lilac, fawn, red, and cream
Personality: Friendly, active, entertaining

Usually tailless but Cymrics can be born with stumpy or full-length tails
Double coat
Round face
Ruff of fur around neck
Muscular and compact body
Front legs are shorter than back legs
Thick fur on back legs makes them look like they're wearing baggy trousers

TONKINESE

Take a dash of the Siamese's sass (p69) and a pinch of the Burmese's beauty (p71) and you get the Tonkinese. Crosses between Siamese and Burmese cats have existed for centuries in Asia, but the modern Tonkinese is the result of a breeding programme in Canada and the USA in the 1960s.

The Tonkinese is a confident and social cat that is happiest being the centre of its human's world. They love to build a bond with a special person and will sweetly chatter away to you with a chirpy meow. While they'll be content spending some quality time on your lap, Tonkineses are brainy cats and like to be kept busy learning tricks, such as 'sit' and 'high five', climbing or playing pouncing games.

CAT STATS
Country: Canada/USA **Coat:** Short, fine coat
Colours and patterns: Various colours and patterns, including brown, blue, red, tabby and tortoiseshell. Usually has darker markings on face, ears, legs and tail
Personality: Outgoing, friendly, talkative

Ears with rounded tips
Large eyes, often a dazzling blue colour
High cheekbones
Silky fur
Compact but elegant body

19

DOMESTIC CATS • NORTH AMERICA

SELKIRK REX

The Selkirk rex is one of several rex breeds, which have wavy, wool-like fur. The origins of this lamb-like cat can be traced to a curly-coated kitten that was adopted from a rescue centre in Montana, USA, in the 1980s. As an adult, she was bred with a Persian (p40) to create kittens that had their mum's curls and their dad's plush fur.

Selkirks are chilled-out souls that love cuddles and keep a kitten-like enthusiasm for playtime well into adulthood. With their calm, happy natures, they are a good choice for families and can live in harmony with cat-friendly dogs, too.

Young Selkirks take a few years to develop their curly coats, and litters can contain wavy- and straight-coated kittens. You can tell if a kitten will have curly hair when it grows up because its whiskers will be curly at birth.

CAT STATS
Country: USA **Coat:** Short or longhaired, thick with loose curls **Colours and patterns:** All colours and patterns **Personality:** Easy-going, loving, social

SOMALI

The stunning Somali is the longhaired cousin of the Abyssinian (p70). Although it is named after a country in Africa, the Somali was developed in the USA in the 1950s, when longhaired kittens started to be born naturally in Abyssinian litters.

While Somalis are charming and friendly, owning one is a bit like inviting a small, demanding panther into your home. These active felines need space to stretch their long legs, and cat trees to show off their climbing skills. Somalis will tolerate chasing a feather on a stick, but games must be inventive to keep them from getting bored and into mischief. If a Somali thinks it is not getting enough attention, it will make a lot of noise to let you know!

CAT STATS
Country: USA **Coat:** Soft, silky long hair
Colours and patterns: Original colour is golden-brown tipped with black; modern varieties include tortoiseshell, silver, blue, chocolate, lilac and cream
Personality: Adventurous, agile, affectionate

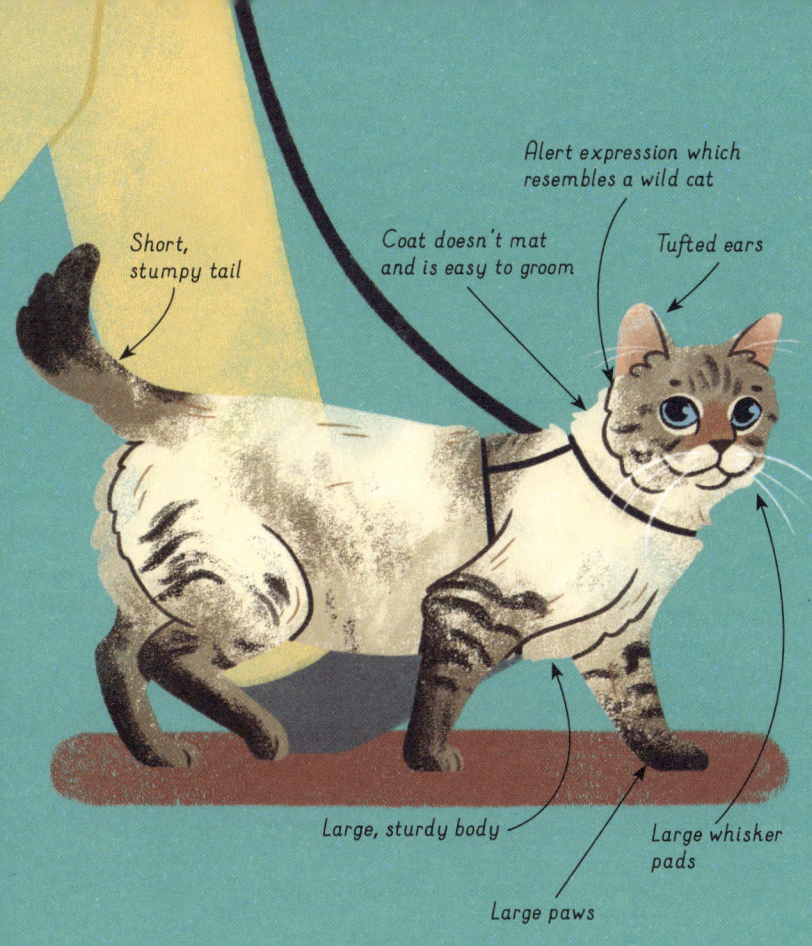

Short, stumpy tail · *Coat doesn't mat and is easy to groom* · *Alert expression which resembles a wild cat* · *Tufted ears* · *Large, sturdy body* · *Large whisker pads* · *Large paws*

AMERICAN BOBTAIL

The ancestors of American bobtails were feral cats with naturally bobbed tails, found throughout the United States. The breed was developed when a couple adopted a stray short-tailed tabby during a holiday to Arizona in the 1960s. They took the cat home to Iowa and he fathered a litter of kittens – all with short tails. This family was the start of the American bobtail breed.

Although they share the same stumpy tail and often tabby-ish markings of America's wild bobcats (p84), bobtails are gentle felines. Sometimes described as dog-like due to their loyal natures and trainability, bobtails can be taught to walk happily on a lead and make affectionate therapy cats and trustworthy family companions.

CAT STATS
Country: USA **Coat:** Short or longhaired
Colours and patterns: All colours and patterns, including tabby, tortoiseshell, chocolate, blue and red **Personality:** Friendly, smart, laid-back

PIXIEBOB

Developed in Washington State in the 1980s, the Pixiebob is another American breed created to look like a wild cat. With its stocky build, tufted ears, short tail and big paws, you could easily mistake one for a wild bobcat or Canada lynx (p84). Despite their tough appearance, Pixiebobs are sweet-natured and adaptable cats that will happily go with the flow in most homes.

Pixiebobs are a 'polydactyl' breed, meaning they often have extra toes. While most cats have five toes on each front foot and four on each back foot, Pixiebobs can have up to seven toes on each foot!

CAT STATS
Country: USA **Coat:** Short or longhaired
Colours and patterns: Brown-spotted tabby
Personality: Devoted, loyal, active

Short tail · *Powerful, robust body* · *Extra toes* · *Tall, tufted ears* · *Spotted tabby pattern on coat, similar to a wild bobcat or lynx* · *Thick coat* · *Thick 'sideburns' around the face*

COURAGEOUS CATS

Some may think that dogs have bounded off with (and probably slobbered all over) every 'hero' award going, but just because cats are independent creatures that doesn't mean they are any less capable of loving and loyal acts. Here are a few stories of courageous and faithful felines that prove just how paw-some cats are.

SIMON

In 1948, a British sailor discovered a scrawny black-and-white cat prowling around the docks in Hong Kong. The sailor brought the stray back to his ship, the HMS *Amethyst*, where the stray was welcomed by the rest of the crew and given the name Simon. The little cat soon made himself at home, patrolling the deck and snoozing in the captain's cabin.

The following year, the HMS *Amethyst* was ordered to sail to Shanghai in China. At the time, China was in the middle of a deadly civil war. The ship was travelling up the Yangtze River when it came under heavy gunfire and became trapped. The captain and 18 sailors were killed during the shooting, and many other members of the crew were badly injured – including Simon.

Huge, hungry rats began to overrun the damaged ship, raiding the food supplies and threatening the health of the crew. Despite being wounded, Simon hunted down the rats, single-pawed, keeping the crew and their supplies safe. The presence of the plucky cat also boosted the men's morale when they were close to giving up hope. When the ship eventually managed to escape 101 days later, 'Able Seacat' Simon was hailed as a hero and awarded the PDSA Dickin Medal, an award given to animals for acts of great bravery and devotion during war. To date, he is the only cat to have received this honour.

FÉLICETTE

On 18 October 1963, a French kitty called Félicette made a giant leap for felinekind when she became the first and, so far, only cat to go into space. Her mission took place in the early days of space technology, when scientists wanted to understand how the lack of gravity (or weightlessness) in space could affect living creatures. Felicétte was sent 160 km (100 miles) above the Earth in a rocket and experienced 5 minutes of weightlessness before being parachuted safely back to land. Today, this heroic astro-cat is commemorated by a statue at the International Space University in Strasbourg, France.

TARA

One spring day in 2014, a four-year-old boy called Jeremy was riding his bike in the driveway of his home in California, USA. Suddenly, a passing dog rushed at Jeremy, pulling him off the bike. The dog may have been quick, but it wasn't as fast as Jeremy's loyal tabby, Tara. As soon as she saw what was happening, Tara leapt on the dog and chased it away, before running back to check on Jeremy. Thanks to Tara's bravery and lightning-quick reaction, the little boy made a full recovery.

MASHA

On a freezing winter's night in Russia in 2015, a tiny baby boy was abandoned in a box in the staircase of a block of flats. Fortunately, it wasn't long before he was found by a gentle longhaired cat called Masha. Hearing the baby's cries, Masha climbed inside the box, wrapped her furry body around the child to keep him warm, and meowed loudly to attract the attention of people living in the building. They rushed the baby to hospital where everyone was relieved to find that he was fit and well, in spite of being in the cold for several hours – all thanks to marvellous Masha.

DOMESTIC CATS · NORTH AMERICA

MAINE COON

Typically measuring up to 1 metre (40 inches) long, the mighty Maine coon is the king of the domestic cats. One of the oldest cat breeds in North America, it is named partly after the New England state of Maine, where it first appeared in the 1850s, and partly for its bushy tail's similarity to the tail of a racoon (or 'coon').

The Maine coon's powerful build, weatherproof coat and excellent hunting skills reflect its humble origins as a farm cat. The ancestors of today's Maine coons had to keep the homestead free from rats and mice and fend for themselves in harsh New England winters.

Maine coons have a quiet voice for such a large cat. They don't tend to meow but make a chirpy, trill-like sound when talking to their humans.

- Big, tufted ears
- Especially shaggy fur on tummy, as added protection from the cold
- Sturdy legs
- Tufts of fur between toes to keep feet warm
- Large paws
- Long, bushy tail

Unsurprisingly, these gentle giants need plenty of room to roam about, so this is not a breed to pick if you want an indoor cat. Although they like their independence, they love to be part of family life, are friendly with other animals and calm with kids. If you want an affectionate, handsome companion and have a big enough sofa, you can't get much better than the magnificent Maine coon.

CAT STATS
Country: USA **Coat:** Long, thick, double coat
Colours and patterns: Various colours and patterns, typically brown, red or silver tabby, classic (marble-like pattern) or mackerel stripes
Personality: Gentle, intelligent, independent

EXOTIC SHORTHAIR

If you've fallen in love with the Persian but can't commit to such a demanding hair-care regime, the exotic shorthair might be the cat for you. This cuddly breed was created in the USA in the 1960s by crossing Persians (p40) with American shorthairs (p28) and Burmese (p71). The result was a cat with the looks and dignified air of the Persian, but with a shorter, more manageable coat. Even so, as a flat-faced breed, exotics struggle to clean themselves properly, so they need a daily brush to keep their coats healthy.

Sociable and sweet, an exotic will happily snooze on your lap for hours. When encouraged, they will get involved in chase and pouncing games, but they are just as content watching the world go by from a sunny windowsill.

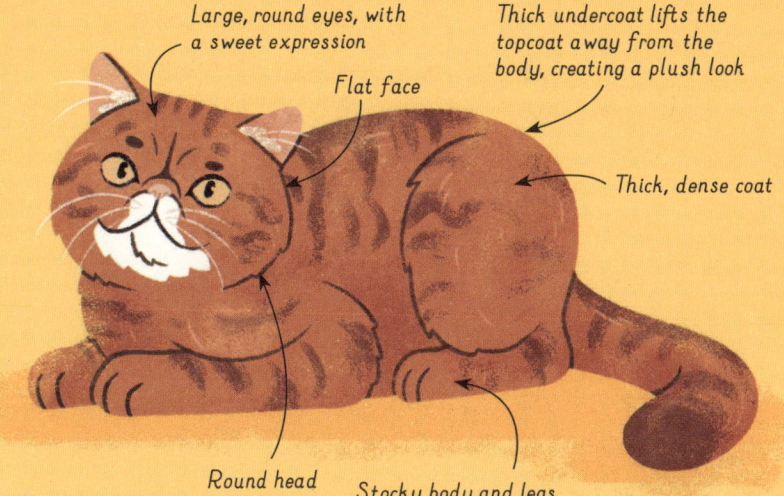

Large, round eyes, with a sweet expression
Flat face
Thick undercoat lifts the topcoat away from the body, creating a plush look
Thick, dense coat
Round head
Stocky body and legs

CAT STATS
Country: USA **Coat:** Medium and plush – slightly longer than most shorthaired cats **Colours and patterns:** All colours and patterns, including white, cream, red, silver, blue and chocolate, and tabby, tortoiseshell and tricolour **Personality:** Good-natured, playful, affectionate

BALINESE

The beautiful Balinese is a longhaired cousin of the short-coated Siamese (p69). Longhaired kittens can appear naturally in Siamese litters and, in the 1950s, two American breeders decided to develop these cats into a breed of their own. The name Balinese was chosen because the graceful movement of these delicate felines reminded the breeders of dancers from Bali (in Indonesia).

Balinese are dazzling cats, but don't be fooled by their soft looks and bewitching blue eyes – they are mischievous creatures that require a committed owner to keep up with them. Fun-loving and curious, Balinese like company and adventures. A climbing tree along with lots of playtime (and chats – they are a noisy breed!) with their favourite human will keep a Balinese happy.

Long, straight nose
Almond-shaped, bright blue eyes
Fine, silky fur with no undercoat, meaning the fur lies flat against the body
Slender body
Fluffy tail
Long, slim legs

CAT STATS
Country: USA **Coat:** Long, fine and silky **Colours and patterns:** Seal, blue, chocolate, lilac, red and cream **Personality:** Clever, loving, talkative

DOMESTIC CATS • NORTH AMERICA

RAGDOLL

These big, beautiful cats are as sweet as their brilliant blue eyes, rabbit-soft fur and dolly-like name suggest. Ragdolls were created by a breeder called Ann Baker in California in the 1960s. Baker's original cats had a tendency to go limp when picked up, a bit like a soft ragdoll toy in a child's arms.

Nowadays, these cuddly cats can be found warming laps the world over and are especially popular in the USA and UK. It's not hard to see why. Ragdolls are exceptionally gentle felines that will willingly be carried around by kids, happily live alongside other pets and never say no to a tummy rub.

Because they are so friendly and chilled-out, ragdolls don't have the street-smart attitude of many other breeds, so shouldn't be allowed to roam outside unsupervised. Fortunately, keeping an eye on a ragdoll isn't hard because their favourite place to be is by your side. Often described as 'dog-like', these loyal felines will follow you from room to room and pick a cosy spot next to you on the sofa over a rooftop adventure any day.

Broad head
Blue eyes
Large, sturdy body
Thick, silky coat
Fluffy tail

CAT STATS

Country: USA **Coat:** Long, soft, silky coat **Colours and patterns:** One of three patterns – colourpoint, bicolour and mitted (with white 'mittens' on feet). Colours are seal, blue, chocolate, lilac, cinnamon, fawn, red and cream along with the tortoiseshell and lynx **Personality:** Friendly, gentle, loving

RAGAMUFFIN

This huggable cat is related to the more well-known ragdoll (see opposite). The ragamuffin came about because breeders wanted to introduce a greater variety of colours and patterns into the ragdoll line – while ragdolls come in three key patterns, anything goes with a ragamuffin. To create the ragamuffin, ragdolls were bred with Persians (p40) and longhaired moggies to make a larger, fluffier cat.

These laid-back cats enjoy being part of the family – from trotting to the door to welcome their humans, to being cuddled by kids and making friends with gentle dogs. Although they love taking it easy (and frequent tummy rubs), playtime with laser lights and toy mice should be encouraged to keep these chunky cats fit.

> **CAT STATS**
> **Country:** USA **Coat:** Long, dense and silky
> **Colours and patterns:** All colours, including chocolate, cream, black, red and silver, and all patterns, including solid, bicolour, tabby and tortoiseshell **Personality:** Affectionate, calm, cuddly

- Triangular ears
- Big eyes that can be various colours, such as blue, green, gold and amber
- Large, muscular body
- Ruff of fur around neck
- Thick, soft, tangle-resistant coat
- Long, plumed tail

SNOWSHOE

In the 1950s, a breeder in Philadelphia found three Siamese kittens with mitten-like markings on their paws. She decided to create a new type of kitty, combining the Siamese (p69) with the American shorthair (p28) to make a cat with a smart coat and feet that look like they've been dipped in icing sugar.

Snowshoes are polite and charming to everyone, though they generally save their affection for one extra-special person in the house. These intelligent cats like to exercise their brains and speedy bodies on cat agility courses. They're also unusually fond of water and will happily splash about in a washing-up bowl or amuse themselves trying to 'catch' a stream from a tap with their dainty paws.

> **CAT STATS**
> **Country:** USA **Coat:** Short and smooth **Colours and patterns:** All Siamese colours (seal, lilac, blue and chocolate) in a pointed pattern, with white feet
> **Personality:** Outgoing, loyal, smart

- Triangular ears
- Blue eyes
- Fairly long, rectangular body
- Muscular, athletic build
- White feet
- Tail, legs, head and ears are darker than the body

DOMESTIC CATS • NORTH AMERICA

AMERICAN SHORTHAIR

The American shorthair is descended from ships' cats that travelled to North America with European settlers in the 1600s. Cats were a common sight on ships, where they were used to keep rats and mice under control, and they would have had a similar job once they set paw in New England on the east coast of North America – a document from 1634 describes how a group of tough moggies saved a colony's crops from hungry squirrels and chipmunks.

These cats developed naturally in the USA for centuries before the breed was established and named in the 1960s. The modern American shorthair is similar in size to the British shorthair (p38) but not quite as chunky.

- Large, round head
- Medium-built, sturdy body
- Short coat that's easily maintained with a weekly brush
- Slightly rounded ear tips
- Short nose
- Strong jaws
- Blunt tail tip

CAT STATS
Country: USA **Coat:** Short and thick **Colours and patterns:** All colours and patterns; most common is tabby **Personality:** Adaptable, good-natured, smart

Like its pioneering ancestors, today's American shorthair is a practical, adaptable feline that can make itself comfy in most households. It will happily take itself off for a snooze on a pile of laundry or amuse itself hunting flies when you're busy, but is always up for playtime or cuddles. The American shorthair makes a great all-round family cat.

AMERICAN WIREHAIR

This sweet-natured cat looks identical to the American shorthair in pretty much every way, apart from its very unusual coat. The first American wirehair was born to a pair of farm cats in upstate New York in 1966. Each hair on an American wirehair bends at the tip, creating a springy coat that feels rough when you stroke it.

An American wirehair's fur requires little grooming – in fact, too much grooming can damage the texture, so a gentle weekly brush is enough to keep it looking its best. Unlike its shorthair cousin, the wirehair isn't a big fan of the outdoors, preferring to lounge on a sunny windowsill or next to a warm radiator rather than risk getting its paws wet.

> **CAT STATS**
> **Country:** USA **Coat:** Short, rough coat **Colours and patterns:** All colours and patterns **Personality:** Friendly, easy-going, playful

Short nose · Broad, round face · Big cheeks · Curly whiskers · Medium-built, sturdy body · Harsh, wiry coat

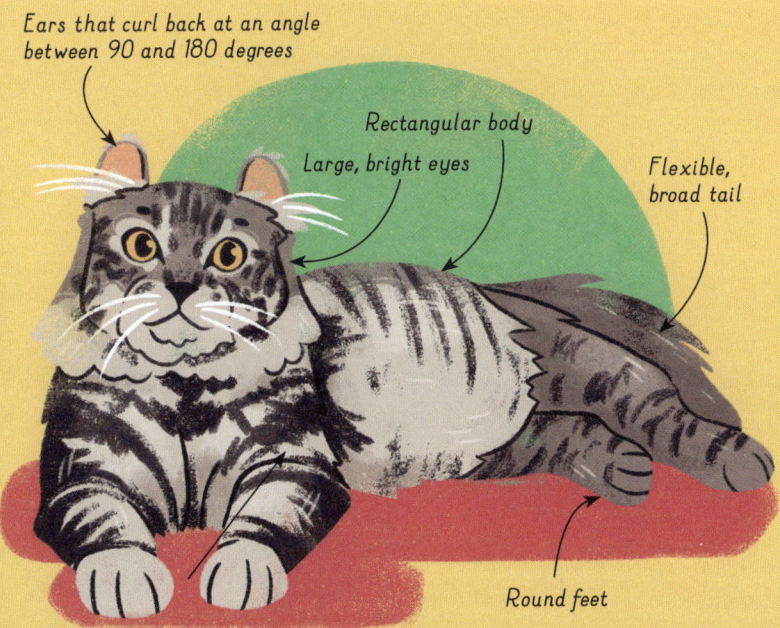

Ears that curl back at an angle between 90 and 180 degrees · Rectangular body · Large, bright eyes · Flexible, broad tail · Round feet

American curl kittens are born with straight ears. Their ears begin to curl after a couple of days and have settled into their adult shape by the time the cat is about 4 months old.

AMERICAN CURL

No other cat looks quite like the American curl. Named for their incredible backwards-turning ears, all American curls are descended from a stray longhaired, curly-eared kitten that turned up on a doorstep in California in 1981.

Curls are cheerful, expressive cats that like to nuzzle and head-bump their owners to show their affection, and chatter away to you with a gentle 'cooing' sound. They are also inquisitive creatures and can use their nimble paws to open doors when exploring. Often nicknamed the 'Peter Pans of the cat world', these cats remain playful and kittenish well into old age.

> **CAT STATS**
> **Country:** USA **Coat:** Short or long **Colours and patterns:** All colours and patterns **Personality:** Fun-loving, curious, friendly

DOMESTIC CATS · NORTH AMERICA

LAPERM

The LaPerm sounds like something you might ask for at the hairdressers, but it is actually a cat with showstopping curly fur. The coats of LaPerms range from tight, bouncy ringlets to loose waves, just like the 'perm' hairdos of the 1980s. The breed was established in the 1980s when a family of cats with curly coats were discovered living on a farm in Oregon.

While a LaPerm will happily be fussed over, it will still chase a ping-pong ball round a room with kittenish enthusiasm and snuggle up to your neck when it's worn out. Their springy locks aren't hard to groom, and there's nothing these cats love more than a good pamper session with their favourite person.

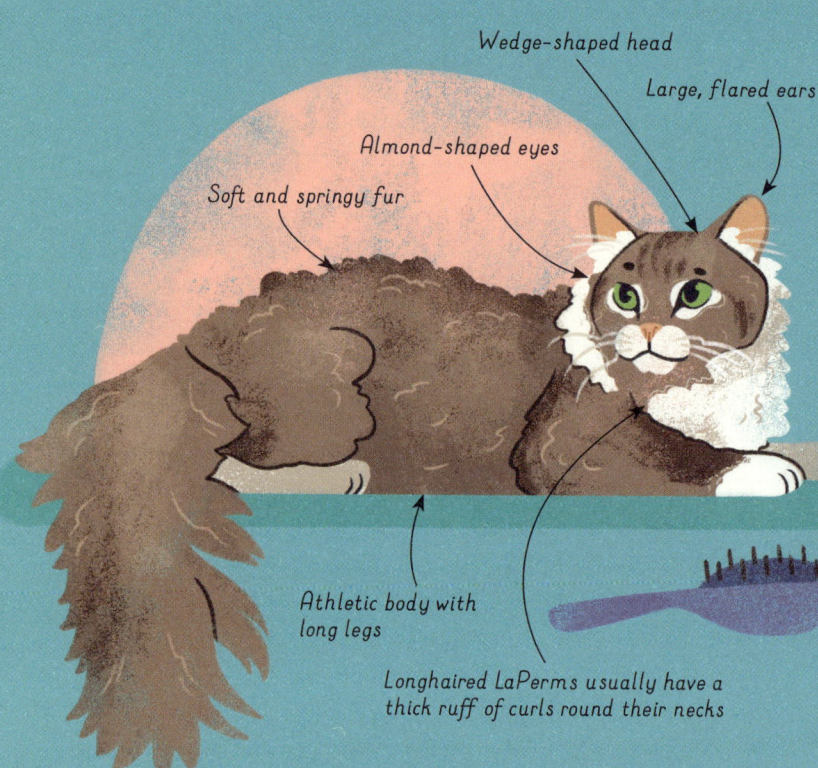

- Wedge-shaped head
- Large, flared ears
- Almond-shaped eyes
- Soft and springy fur
- Athletic body with long legs
- Longhaired LaPerms usually have a thick ruff of curls round their necks

These cats are cuddle bugs! When held, they will reach for your face with their paws and gently nuzzle you.

CAT STATS
Country: USA **Coat:** Short or long, with tight or loose soft curls **Colours and patterns:** All colours and patterns, including black, blue, fawn, tabby, chocolate, tortoiseshell and tricolour **Personality:** Loving, easy-going, playful

LYKOI

Whether you find this feline adorable or like something out of a bad dream, there's no denying that the lykoi, or 'werewolf cat', has a look of its own. A very recent breed, the lykoi was established in Virginia in the 2010s by breeders who noticed that some of the local feral cats had an unusual, partially hairless coat.

What hair lykois have is very soft and fine, with white hairs scattered throughout. Underneath that wolfish appearance is a clever and playful cat with a particularly strong hunting instinct – games that involve lots of pouncing and stalking are sure to be a hit with a lively lykoi.

- Usually has a hairless 'mask' that connects the muzzle to the ears and eyes
- Large, wide ears, usually hairless
- Gold-coloured eyes
- Slender body
- Thin tail
- Wedge-shaped head
- Long, agile toes

The cat was named after the Greek word 'lykos', which means 'wolf'.

CAT STATS
Country: USA **Coat:** Short and fine **Colours and patterns:** Roan – a solid base colour (black or brown) with white highlights **Personality:** Smart, active, friendly

MUNCHKIN

The munchkin is the sausage dog of the cat world. Despite their low-slung stature, they're busy and active creatures that love to play with their humans. Inquisitive by nature, a munchkin has a sweet habit of sitting up on its back legs like a rabbit when something catches its eye.

Short-legged cats have appeared naturally around the world for centuries, but it wasn't until the 1980s that the munchkin was established as a breed. Although the munchkin is an accepted breed in the USA, many cat associations in other parts of the world do not encourage breeding short-legged cats because of health concerns.

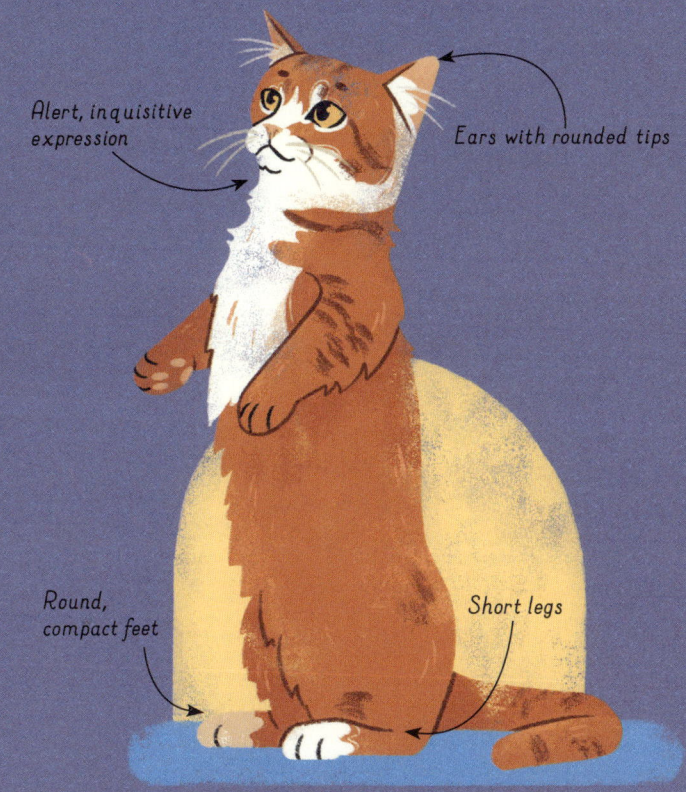

Alert, inquisitive expression
Ears with rounded tips
Round, compact feet
Short legs

CAT STATS
Country: USA **Coat:** Short or long **Colours and patterns:** All colours and patterns, including black, blue, chocolate, cream, lilac, red, tabby and tricolour
Personality: Gentle, curious, smart

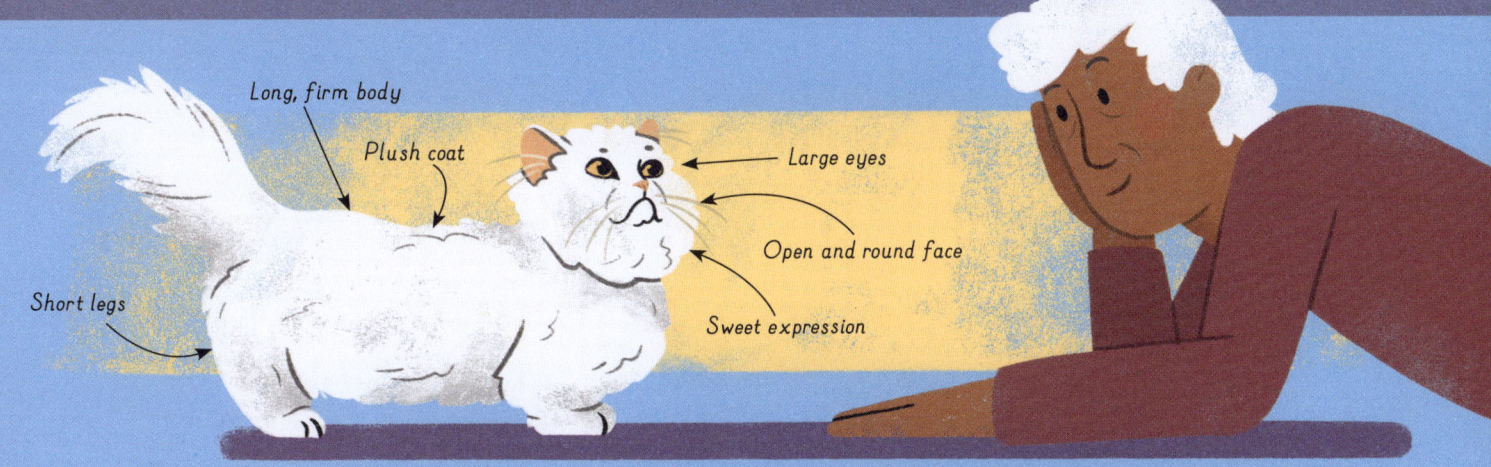

Long, firm body
Plush coat
Large eyes
Open and round face
Sweet expression
Short legs

MINUET

The minuet is one of several variations of the munchkin (see above) created in the 1990s by crossing that breed with Persians (p40). While they have cute personalities and a roly-poly charm, minuets are not common outside of the USA due to possible health problems such as arthritis.

Combining the playfulness of the munchkin with the sweetness of the Persian, a minuet will happily accept lap-warming duties and generally want to be wherever you are. These people-loving cats adore company and aren't suited to being left alone for long periods. They're happiest being doted on by a gentle family or a single owner.

CAT STATS
Country: USA **Coat:** Short or long **Colours and patterns:** All colours and patterns, including white, blue, chocolate, tabby and tortoiseshell
Personality: Laid-back, cuddly, gentle

DOMESTIC CATS · NORTH AMERICA

BENGAL

Although the Bengal has only been around since the 1990s, it has prowled its way into hearts and homes all over the globe. It was developed by crossing hybrid cats (mixes between a leopard cat [p99] and a domestic tabby) with breeds such as the Abyssinian (p70), Burmese (p71) and Egyptian mau (p50). The aim was to create a gentle cat with stunning leopard-like looks in order to discourage people from buying wild cats as pets.

Bengals are adaptable, affectionate and amusing cats. They love water and are enchanted by the sight of a running tap or a loo flushing! While they enjoy being close to their humans, Bengals will not stay still on a lap for long – they have busy brains, need space to run, jump and play and, if kept indoors, they need climbing trees, boxes and tunnels to explore.

Broad, wedge-shaped head

Strong, elegant body

Some Bengals lack colour in the tips of their hairs, which give their coats a 'glittery' look

Spotted or marbled coat

Back legs are slightly longer than front legs

CAT STATS
Country: USA **Coat:** Short, dense and silky
Colours and patterns: Brown, blue, silver and snow in spotted or marbled tabby patterns
Personality: Sociable, loving, energetic

Because of their size and hunting instincts, it is not normally a good idea to let these cats outside unsupervised. If you can provide a Bengal with an outdoor cat run or a cat-proof garden, they'll be very happy. Or, better yet, these clever cats can be trained to wear a harness and lead, so you can take a walk on the wild side with your mini leopard in safety.

OCICAT

If you want the beauty of a wild cat in a friendly and entirely tame package, look no further than the ocicat. This affectionate cat was created in the 1960s when a breeder crossed a Siamese (p69) with an Abyssinian (p70). The sturdiness of the American shorthair (p28) was later added into the mix to make a well-balanced and loving companion.

Like their Siamese cousins, ocicats adore spending time with their humans. They are smart kitties that can quickly learn commands and have a puppy-like enjoyment of fetch and tug games. When you have to get some homework done, puzzle feeders and robotic mouse toys are a great way to keep this would-be wild cat out of mischief.

> **CAT STATS**
> **Country:** USA **Coat:** Short and satin-like
> **Colours and patterns:** Six colours with a tabby pattern. These colours are: tawny, chocolate, cinnamon, blue, lilac and fawn. Ocicats can also be any of these colours with a silver background
> **Personality:** Smart, playful, outgoing

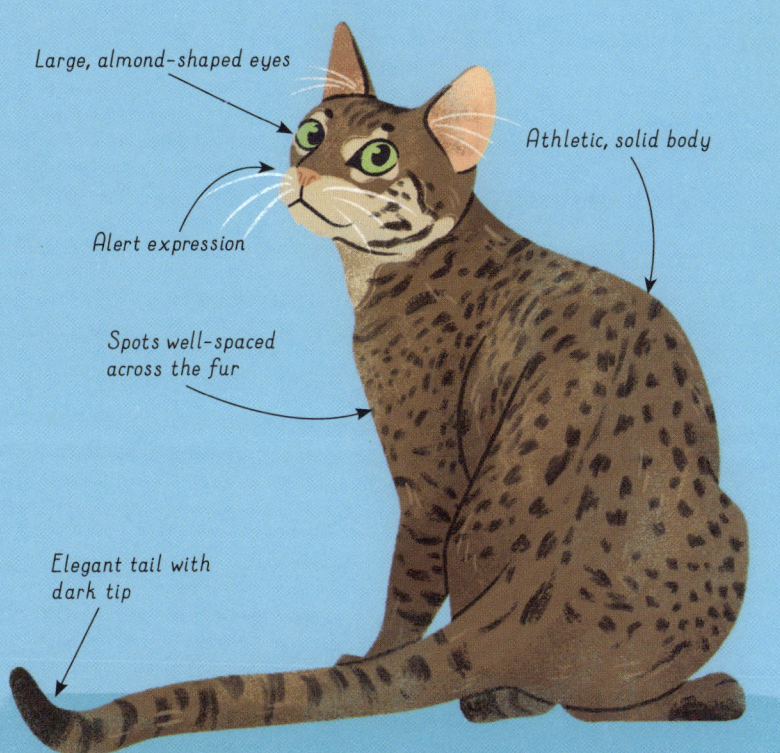

- Large, almond-shaped eyes
- Athletic, solid body
- Alert expression
- Spots well-spaced across the fur
- Elegant tail with dark tip

The breed was named 'ocicat' because of the cats' resemblance to the wild ocelot (p87). However, no wild cats were involved in the creation of the breed.

TOYGER

Watch this powerful, stripy puss stalk through a kitchen and you could be forgiven for thinking a tiger has dropped by for tea. Although it wouldn't look out of place in a jungle, the toyger was created in the USA in the 1990s by crossing a Bengal cat (see opposite) with a household tabby.

Unlike a wild tiger (p96), the toyger is a social creature that wants to be part of the family and won't be happy spending lots of time alone. These intelligent and outgoing cats love exercise and bonding with their humans, making them an especially good breed for feline agility.

- Round eyes
- Small, rounded ears
- Prominent whisker pads
- Large, long body, carried low to the ground like a big cat
- Banded, stripy markings which resemble a wild tiger's

> **CAT STATS**
> **Country:** USA **Coat:** Short, dense and soft
> **Colours and patterns:** Brown, mackerel and tabby
> **Personality:** Even-tempered, clever, confident

CAT SHOWS

If you want to meet the top kitties in town, get yourself down to a cat show. This is an event where breeders (known as 'cat fanciers') and owners can take their cats and win prizes. But you don't need to have a cat to be part of the action. Attending a show is a great way to learn about the world of cats and meet some marvellous breeds and moggies.

UP TO SCRATCH?

Preparation for a cat show involves weeks of brushing, bathing and health checks, so breeders can make sure their cats look and feel purr-fect on the big day. When a breeder arrives at the show, they take their cat to a pen. The judges will either visit the cats there or take them to a judging table to be assessed. A judge inspects a cat by picking it up and handling it, before giving a mark. Pedigree show cats are judged on how closely they match the official description of their breed (called a 'breed standard'). Pet cats or crossbreeds are judged in a more relaxed way based on their health and temperament – the friendlier and cuddlier the better! Rosettes, silver cups and other prizes are on offer for the cats that score the highest marks.

BATH TIME!

The amount of time an owner spends grooming their show cat varies from breed to breed – a longhaired cat will require more preparation than a shorthaired cat, for example. But whatever length the cat's hair, all show cats will have a bath before their big day. This pamper session usually involves several shampoos and rinses – at least one to remove any grease and dirt from the cat's fur, and another to condition and thicken the coat. The cat will then be combed, blow-dried and brushed, its face, eyes and ears will be wiped clean, and the tips of its claws trimmed as a final touch.

THE HISS-TORY OF CAT SHOWS

Cat shows were set up during the 19th century, when there was a growing interest in breeding all sorts of animals for particular looks or personalities – a process called 'selective breeding'. The first official cat show took place in London in 1871, and the first cat show in the USA happened in New York in 1895. Today, these events take place all over the world. They are normally run by cat breeders' associations, which set rules about breeds and how shows should be run.

Some shows feature cat agility competitions. Super-fast felines whizz through an obstacle course of hoops, jumps and tunnels to win a prize.

FELINE GOOD

If you're thinking of entering your own cat in a show, it's important that it enjoys taking part. Some cats lap up attention, but if your cat is shy, it probably won't like the noisy show hall or being picked up by a stranger. And an active cat won't want to sit in a pen most of the day!

Thanks to its fancy, floofy fur, the Persian has won 'Best in Show' at the USA's Cat Fanciers' Association International Cat Show more times than any other breed.

EUROPE & AFRICA
Domestic Breeds

Cats have long reigned supreme on the continents of Europe and Africa. Africa is where our love for domestic cats first kicked off, while Europe was where the craze for creating breeds began in the 19th century. Cats from this part of the world range from stately pusses that like to survey their kingdoms from a sofa to stealthy felines that are most at home patrolling a forest. Let's meet them!

The earliest known remains of a domestic cat, which date back 9,500 years, were discovered on the island of Cyprus in the early 2000s.

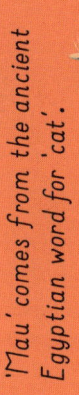

12.

No one is sure how Chartreux cats got their name. One theory is that they were named after the Chartreuse monastery, where they were the companions of monks. Another is that the rich texture of their fur reminded people of 'pile de Chartreux', a type of Spanish wool.

11.

10.

Fashion designer Karl Lagerfeld owned a Birman named Choupette. This pampered puss lived a lavish lifestyle with her owner, dining on freshly prepared meals each night and travelling around the world with her own bodyguard and personal assistant.

16.

'Mau' comes from the ancient Egyptian word for 'cat'.

17.

DOMESTIC CATS · EUROPE & AFRICA

BRITISH SHORTHAIR

Take one look at the adorably smiley face of the British shorthair and it's easy to see why this cat is the most popular pedigree breed in the UK. First recorded as a breed in 1870, its origins are thought to date back to the Roman invasion of Britain from c. 43 CE, when sturdy mousers were brought over from Italy and bred with native British cats.

Today, the British shorthair is a calm and well-mannered ruler of many a household. A stately soul, this compact cat likes to keep its paws on the ground when patrolling its empire, rather than be carried around. If you respect this, you will be rewarded with a devoted companion that will enjoy snuggles beside you on the sofa.

British shorthairs love a good catnap and can be lazy, especially as they get older. Coupled with the breed's chunky build, this means these cats can get overweight. To keep them in shape, it's important to encourage exercise through gentle play or 'scatter feeding' their meals – hiding small portions of biscuits around a feeding area or climbing tower to encourage the cat to 'hunt' for food.

A British shorthair tabby is thought to have been the inspiration for the grinning Cheshire Cat in 'Alice's Adventures in Wonderland'.

A blue coat with bright orange eyes is the classic look.

Plush fur with an unusual 'crisp' texture

Smiley expression

Large head with prominent cheeks

Medium-length tail with rounded tip

Short, sturdy legs

CAT STATS
Country: UK **Coat:** Short and dense, with a crisp texture **Colours and patterns:** Various, including solid blue, grey, cream and red, bicolour, colourpoint, tipped, tortoiseshell and tabby **Personality:** Patient, trusting, laid-back

It's a good idea to introduce British longhair kittens to hairbrushes and being groomed, so they feel comfortable with the process before they grow their full, fabulous adult coat.

- Large whisker pads
- Fluffy ruff around neck
- Longer fur on back legs
- Brush-like tail
- Large, round paws
- Strong legs

BRITISH LONGHAIR

If you've fallen in love with the British shorthair (see opposite) but want a cat on the fluffier side, say hello to the British longhair. Although only recently recognised as a breed in the UK, the British longhair has its roots in the first half of the 20th century. At that time, Persians (p40) and Turkish Angoras (p59) were being bred with British shorthairs in an attempt to give the cats rounder and flatter faces. As a result, some longhaired kittens started to appear in British shorthair litters.

This cat's stand-out feature is its gorgeous flowing coat, which needs grooming daily to keep it tangle-free and spectacular. Hair-care aside, the British longhair is an undemanding cat that is pretty much identical to the British shorthair in temperament.

Mild-mannered and affectionate, these cats take their time over things and enjoy leisurely days filled with plenty of snoozing, eating and the occasional pounce after a feather toy. Being sensitive souls, they prefer calm households where there isn't too much going on and they can be admired by their human subjects.

CAT STATS
Country: UK **Coat:** Long and dense
Colours and patterns: Various, including solid blue, grey, cream and red, bicolour, colourpoint, tipped, tortoiseshell and tabby **Personality:** Loving, quiet, even-tempered

DOMESTIC CATS · EUROPE & AFRICA

PERSIAN

With its stately expression and cloud of soft fur, the Persian is a true aristo-cat. Persians were probably developed from cats that were brought to Europe in the 1600s from Afghanistan and Iran (which used to be called Persia). The modern breed was purr-fected in the UK in the 19th century, and the cats quickly padded their way on to the laps of the wealthy and well-to-do – Britain's Queen Victoria owned two blue Persians.

Persians are showstopper cats and they know it. Their thick coats come in a variety of colours and require daily brushing to keep them looking their best. Despite their demanding hair-care regime, these cats have easy-going characters and form strong bonds with their owners.

Persians used to have longer noses but the modern breed has been exaggerated to create cats with very flat faces. This can cause health problems, including breathing difficulties. Don't expect lots of running about from a Persian – these distinguished cats like to take things at a relaxed pace. Persians are happiest living in a calm household with a cosy cushion from which they can survey their kingdom.

- Round head with short nose
- Large, expressive eyes
- Compact body
- Small ears
- Bushy tail
- Dense, double-coated fur (many types of Persian have a thick ruff round their neck and shoulders)
- Sturdy legs with large paws

CAT STATS

Country: Origins uncertain, but developed as a breed in the UK and Europe **Coat:** Long, thick and silky **Colours and patterns:** A variety of colours, including black, white, chocolate, silver, golden, red, blue and lilac. Patterns include colourpoint, bicolour, tricolour, tortoiseshell and tabby **Personality:** Gentle, dignified, quiet

SCOTTISH FOLD

The Scottish fold can trace its origins to a cat called Susie who had unusual folded ears and was discovered on a farm in Scotland in the 1960s. Susie's descendants were bred with Persians (p40), British shorthairs (p38) and American shorthairs (p28) to create this rare breed with a teddy-bear face and a sweet nature. Perhaps thanks to their barnyard ancestors, Scottish folds are hardy and adaptable as well as loving, making them great cats for families.

All Scottish folds are born with straight ears. If a kitten carries the folded-ear gene, its ears will begin to fold forwards when it is around 4 weeks old. Some Scottish fold kittens have un-folded ears and are known as 'Scottish straights' (see kitten in picture on the left). The gene that causes folded ears can lead to bone problems, so Scottish folds must be bred carefully so the cats stay happy and healthy.

- Ears that fold forwards
- Big, round eyes
- Dense, plush coat
- Rounded body
- Dainty paws

Pop star Taylor Swift is the proud owner of two Scottish folds called Olivia Benson and Meredith Grey.

CAT STATS
Country: UK **Coat:** Short and dense, or longhaired **Colours and patterns:** Most colours and patterns, including blue, red, tabby and tortoiseshell **Personality:** Loyal, playful, curious

MANX

Legend has it that an unlucky ancestor of the Manx cat was the last animal to leave Noah's Ark and got its tail caught in the door. In reality, the Manx can trace its tailless-ness to a population of short-tailed cats on the Isle of Man off the west coast of Britain sometime before the 18th century. The cats developed in isolation from their long-tailed cousins on mainland Britain and the unique Manx breed was born.

These chunky cats may look like couch potatoes but they are excellent hunters and jumpers, thanks to their particularly powerful back legs (another legend claims they are cats crossed with rabbits). In the past, they made popular ship and farm cats. Today, they make acrobatic and amusing companions, who will enjoy putting their busy brains to use playing string games or even fetch with you.

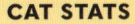

- A 'rumpy' Manx has a hollow where the tail should be.
- A 'stumpy' Manx has a very short tail.
- Double coat
- Large ears
- Full cheeks
- Strong back legs that are longer than the front legs
- Compact and sturdy body

CAT STATS
Country: UK **Coat:** Short, double coat
Colours and patterns: Most colours and patterns, including black, red, tabby and tricolour
Personality: Intelligent, active, social

Manx cats are famous for having no tail, but litters of Manx kittens can include cats with stumpy tails or full-length tails.

DOMESTIC CATS · EUROPE & AFRICA

CORNISH REX

Known as the feline greyhound, the Cornish rex is a slim, speedy cat that loves to gallop around on its long legs. The comparison to dogs doesn't end there – these people-loving kitties crave human company and enjoy a game of fetch, sometimes using their agile paws to pick up toys.

But what really sets this breed apart is its gorgeous crinkly coat. All Cornish rex cats can trace their curls to a kitten called Kallibunker, who was born in Cornwall, UK, in 1950 and had unusual crimped hair. When Kallibunker had curly coated kittens of his own, they were bred with Siamese (p69), Russian blues (p56) and British (p38) and American shorthairs (p28) to create this one-of-a-kind breed.

CAT STATS
Country: UK **Coat:** Short, dense, curly coat
Colours and patterns: All colours and patterns, including black, lilac, brown, red, cream, tabby and tortoiseshell **Personality:** Sweet, social, active

DEVON REX

A tin mine in Devon, UK, is a strange place for a breed of cat to be created, but the Devon rex is not your average feline. In the 1960s, the mine was home to a stray cat with curly fur. He had a litter with a local cat and one of these kittens, called Kirlee, inherited the same wavy coat.

The Devon rex has a busy, nimble personality to match its elfish looks. These cats have a monkey-like love of climbing and will make it their business to explore every shelf, nook and cranny in their home. When a Devon rex is not on a high-flying adventure, you'll probably find this affectionate kitty perched on your shoulder.

CAT STATS
Country: UK **Coat:** Short, soft and curly
Colours and patterns: Any colour and pattern
Personality: Agile, inquisitive, affectionate

SUFFOLK

Established in 2014, the Suffolk is related to an older breed called the Havana, which also had sleek brown fur and bewitching green eyes. This elegant cat doesn't let its chic looks go to its head. Underneath that glossy coat is a down-to-earth kitty that will eagerly run to meet you at the door, play for hours on end and may even attempt to restyle your hair (they love to play with hair).

As kittens, Suffolks rarely use their claws and often clumsily fall off things. This gentleness continues into adulthood – Suffolks are patient and trustworthy felines and especially good companions for kids.

CAT STATS
Country: UK **Coat:** Short and smooth
Colours and patterns: Chocolate or lilac
Personality: Chatty, loving, inquisitive

SEYCHELLOIS

The Seychellois was first developed in the UK in the 1980s by crossing a tortoiseshell-and-white Persian (p40) with a Siamese (p69). The breeder was inspired after reading a description of cats found on the Seychelles islands off the coast of East Africa, which had distinctive white patches on their coats.

As it's a very rare type of cat, not a great deal is known about the Seychellois. Those who have been lucky enough to meet one describe these cats as sociable, softly spoken and devoted. Their Yoda-like ears add to their unusual charm.

CAT STATS
Country: UK **Coat:** Semi-long and fine
Colours and patterns: White with solid, tortoiseshell and tabby markings
Personality: Clever, affectionate, outgoing

CUTE KITTENS

Snuggly, squeaky and mischievous, kittens are all-round adorable. These fluffballs go through some incredible changes in the first few months of life, and they have a lot to pack into their first year so they can grow into happy and settled adult cats. Let's follow a kitten for a year and see what she gets up to.

Just born: 0-3 weeks

Meet Cleo. This tiny kitten has just been born. Her eyes and ears are closed, and she can't stand up on her little legs yet. Cleo crawls on her tummy to get close to her mum so she can keep warm and have a drink of milk. Her mum's milk contains nutrients that will keep Cleo healthy and help her grow. After two weeks, her eyes and ears will open, her baby teeth start to appear, and she'll take her first wobbly steps.

Newborn kittens are cat-napping pros. They spend about 90 per cent of their day snoozing.

Playtime and pouncing: 4-7 weeks

At 4 weeks old, Cleo is steadier on her paws and is starting to play with her brothers and sisters. If she's feeling brave, she may even have a go at pouncing. Her teeth are growing and soon Cleo will be ready to have her first taste of solid kitten food. By seven weeks, her eyes will have changed from baby blue to their adult colour – Cleo's are a brilliant green. She's also old enough to start learning an essential skill – using the litter tray!

A new home: 8-12 weeks

Over the last few weeks, Cleo has played lots with her siblings and her mum, gaining important social skills. She's also been gently stroked and played with by the humans in the house to build her confidence around people. Once she's had her first vaccinations, which will protect her from common cat diseases, and has been microchipped, Cleo's ready to leave her mum and go to her fur-ever human family. She's not going alone – her brother Charlie is coming, too!

Cats usually have between four and six kittens in a litter.

Double trouble: 12-18 weeks

Cleo and Charlie are having fun exploring their new home – there are so many places to hide and climb! Their humans are building a bond with the kittens by playing with them and establishing a regular routine that makes them feel secure. When the kittens are around 16 weeks old, they will have another trip to the vet to be neutered. Cats can start to have kittens of their own at this age, so it's important Cleo and Charlie are neutered to avoid unwanted litters.

Outside adventures: 6-12 months

By six months, Cleo and Charlie are almost fully grown and can start exploring the world beyond the kitchen window – they're very excited! To prepare the kittens for going outside, their owners have taught Cleo and Charlie to come when they call their names and cat-proofed their garden to make sure there aren't any hazards. They'll keep an eye on the kittens for the next couple of weeks while they get used to exploring the big wide world.

It's often recommended that kittens go to homes in pairs rather than on their own. This way, they always have a friend and playmate and can stay well socialised.

Happy Purr-thday: 12 months

Happy birthday, Cleo and Charlie! The kittens are one year old and celebrating with lots of cuddles and catnip mice (a toy filled with a herb called catnip, which cats love!). They still have a kittenish side and go silly when they spot a fly or a ball of string, but they've grown into confident young cats and much-loved members of their human family.

DOMESTIC CATS • EUROPE & AFRICA

BIRMAN

Legend tells how these beautiful cats can be traced to a temple in ancient Burma (now Myanmar) in Southeast Asia. When the temple's priest was attacked by robbers he was protected by his loyal white cat. As a reward for its devotion, a goddess transformed the cat's white fur to gold and its eyes to sapphires. She left its paws white to symbolise its pure heart.

Birmans probably are descended from Southeast Asian cats, but the modern breed was first recorded and developed in France in 1925 ('Birmanie' is the French name for Burma). As if being blessed by a goddess wasn't enough, these cats have a wonderful temperament to match their stunning looks.

Cuddlers rather than hunters, Birmans love to be with – or preferably be sitting on – their people and will chatter away to you with gentle, mew-like noises. A Birman takes pride in its role as your sidekick, playfully picking up pencils or socks in an attempt to be helpful. Peaceful, friendly and fairly easy to care for thanks to their silky, non-matting coats, these fabulous fluffsters make great companions for older people as well as families.

Broad, rounded head

Blue eyes with sweet expression

Ruff around neck

Fluffy tail

All Birmans have a pointed coat – a light-coloured body with darker fur on the legs, tail and facial features

White paws, which look as though the cat is wearing dainty gloves

CAT STATS
Country: France **Coat:** Long and silky **Colours and patterns:** Various colours, including seal, blue, lilac, chocolate, red and cream. All coats have a pointed pattern. **Personality:** Gentle, affectionate, outgoing

CHARTREUX

A very old breed, it's thought the ancestors of today's Chartreux were brought to France from Turkey and Iran by merchants trading along the Silk Road in the 13th century. What happened to these felines for the next 700 years is unclear, but they certainly had a tough time as mousers and street cats, and many were sadly killed for their extremely soft, wool-like fur. By the start of 20th century, only a small number were left, so a group of fans set about saving the cat and establishing the breed. Chartreux are still agile creatures that enjoy playtime, but, maybe because of all those centuries living life by a whisker, they are happiest with a steady routine and a nice cosy pillow to chill out on.

- Wide, round head
- Large eyes, ranging from yellow to copper in colour
- Big cheeks
- Full whisker pads and a firm chin give the cat a smiling expression
- Grey nose
- Sturdy body with deep chest
- Blue lips
- Pink paw pads

Chartreux are clever kitties that can quickly learn how to open doors and even turn on radios!

CAT STATS
Country: France **Coat:** Short and dense with a wool-like texture **Colours and patterns:** Blue-grey **Personality:** Thoughtful, calm, intelligent

APHRODITE

In the 4th century, the island of Cyprus in the Mediterranean Sea was hit by a terrible plague of snakes. A shipload of plucky cats was sent over from Egypt and Palestine to deal with the problem, and they made the island their home. Today, the descendants of these brave felines can be seen roaming the island's streets and sunning themselves on its ancient ruins. In 2006, a breeding programme was set up to preserve the unique look and character of these semi-wild kitties – the result was the Aphrodite cat. True to its snake-busting roots, the Aphrodite is a strong and powerful cat, but it has a sweet, silly nature and spends more time snuggling than snake hunting these days.

- Big and powerful yet elegant body
- Fairly large ears
- Soft, woolly coat, with a thick undercoat in winter
- Olive-shaped eyes
- Back legs slightly longer than front

These hefty kitties are sometimes called the 'Aphrodite giant'. Adult males can weigh up to 8 kg (18 lb).

CAT STATS
Country: Cyprus **Coat:** Short or long **Colours and patterns:** Most colours and patterns, including white, grey, red, black, tabby and tortoiseshell **Personality:** Loyal, social, athletic

DOMESTIC CATS • EUROPE & AFRICA

GERMAN REX

Like other rex cats (see p20 and p42), this rare breed is distinguished by its unique fur. All German rexes are descended from a curly-coated stray that lived in a hospital garden in Berlin just after World War II (1939–1945). In 1951, the cat was adopted by a doctor and named Lammchen (little lamb). Lammchen went on to have several litters of kittens, and many of them shared her wavy hair.

German rex cats were introduced to Cornish rex breeding programmes in the 1960s to improve the health of the Cornish breed. While this helped the Cornish rex to become stronger and more popular, the German rex is now very rare, even in Germany.

German rexes are gentle, cheerful, cuddly cats. They crave company and are happiest living in homes where they can get lots of attention. Although slender and delicate-looking, German rexes are athletic kitties that adore climbing, jumping and games of fetch.

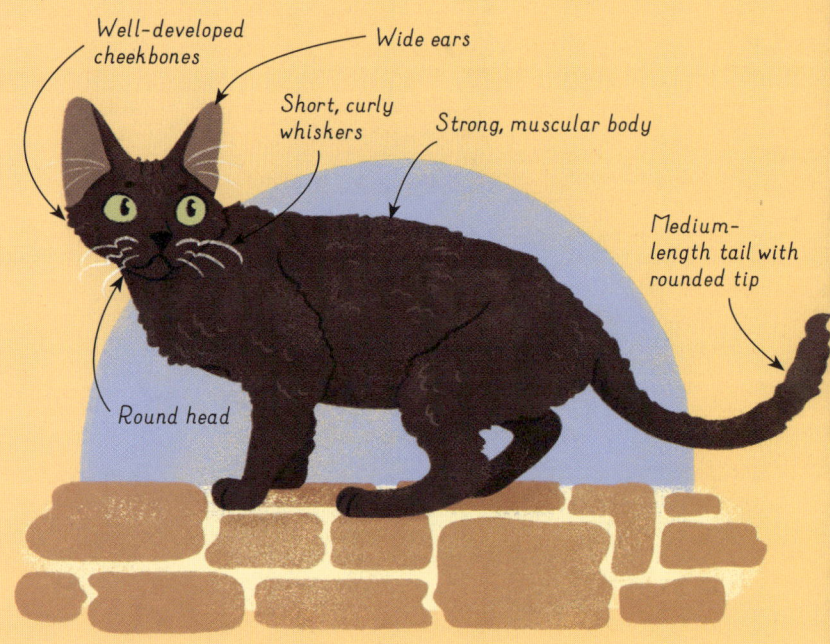

CAT STATS
Country: Germany **Coat:** Short, velvety and curly
Colours and patterns: All colours and patterns, including black, white, red, lilac and cinnamon, and tabby and tortoiseshell **Personality:** Agile, playful, devoted

EUROPEAN SHORTHAIR

You might think this cat looks like any old moggie – and you'd be right! This breed is a pedigree version of domestic cats found across Europe. Like the British shorthair (p38), the European shorthair can trace its roots to the ancient Romans, who used cats to keep their camps clear of rodents as they travelled across the continent. In the 20th century, Swedish breeders decided to preserve the look of Europe's loyal house cats and created an official breed.

Because they were left to their own devices for thousands of years, living as farm mousers and alley cats as well as pets, today's European shorthairs are healthy, hardy felines. Unfussy and affectionate, they make excellent family cats.

While the European shorthair has its origins in Sweden, it is a particularly popular breed in Finland and was named the country's national cat in 2017.

CAT STATS
Country: Sweden **Coat:** Short and dense
Colours and patterns: Various colours, including solid black, blue, cream, red and smoke, and various patterns, including colourpoint, tabby and tortoiseshell
Personality: Independent, calm, adaptable

Norwegian forest cats are larger-than-average felines. Adult males can weigh up to 9 kg (20 lbs) when fully grown — that's twice as heavy as your average house cat. They can be fierce, too, and have been known to chase off foxes!

- Dense coat – thicker in winter than in summer
- Big, tufted ears
- Triangular head with a straight nose
- Large, expressive almond-shaped eyes
- Long, flowing tail
- Strong claws for extra grip when tree- and rock-climbing
- Thick ruff around neck
- Muscular and strong body

NORWEGIAN FOREST CAT

Called the *skogkatt* in its home country and affectionately known as the 'wegie' elsewhere, the Norwegian forest cat has a history as long and rich as its magnificent coat. It's thought that the Vikings originally brought cats to Scandinavia, possibly from Britain and Turkey. Let loose in Norway's deep forests, the cats lived a semi-wild existence, developing powerful bodies, thick waterproof fur and a double coat to protect them during the harsh winter months.

These clever, rugged cats were prized by local people. They were used to patrol farms, villages and ships, keeping food stores safe from rodents with their supreme hunting skills. They also appear in Norwegian folklore as the companions of a goddess (p91) and as 'troll cats', magical, mountain-dwelling felines.

Like their forest-dwelling ancestors, wegies have a deep love of climbing and think nothing of scooting down a tree head first. Although made for an outdoor lifestyle, they will adapt to an indoor set-up if climbing trees or suitable furniture are provided so they can show off their acrobatic skills.

CAT STATS
Country: Norway **Coat:** Long and thick double coat
Colours and patterns: Various colours including white, black, blue, red and cream, and tabby, tortoiseshell, smoke and bicolour patterns
Personality: Loving, intelligent, active

49

DOMESTIC CATS · EUROPE & AFRICA

EGYPTIAN MAU

The pharaoh of the feline world, this elegant breed was the brainwave of a Russian aristocrat in the 1950s. She wanted to create a cat that looked like the spotty felines depicted in ancient Egyptian wall art, tiptoeing between the feet of kings and queens. She took cats straight from the streets of Egypt to develop the breed, so it is quite possible that the melodic purrs of this kitty's ancestors once echoed between the pyramids.

The Egyptian mau has two distinctive sides to its personality. Alert and athletic, it is a playful breed and one of the quickest domestic cats in the world – these fast-footed felines have been recorded hitting speeds of 48 km (30 miles) per hour!

At the same time, it has a sweet and slightly reserved character. Devoted to its human family, the Egyptian mau likes to curl up in a warm lap after a good zooming session, and will show its affection by tenderly kneading you with its delicate paws.

Many Egyptian maus love to play with water and will happily supervise you doing the washing up. These clever cats can even learn to turn taps on and off!

Face markings give the cat a distinctive 'worried' look

Bright green eyes

Graceful, athletic body

Spotted fur

Like many tabbies, Egyptian maus often have stripes on their head that form an 'M' pattern. Some mau fans say that these markings look like a scarab beetle, an important symbol in ancient Egypt.

CAT STATS

Country: Egypt **Coat:** Short and dense **Colours and patterns:** Bronze, silver and smoke, with spotted markings **Personality:** Playful, gentle, loyal

Small head

Large and expressive eyes

Whip-like tail

High cheekbones

Slender body with long legs

SOKOKE

Meet the rarest breed of cat in the world – the Sokoke. This cat is named after the Arabuko Sokoke Forest in Kenya, East Africa, where a group of tabbies with unusual markings lived a semi-wild life among the tropical trees. In the 1970s, a breeder adopted two kittens from the forest and decided to establish the cats as an official breed, to preserve their special look and characteristics.

Sokokes are known locally in Kenya as *kadzonzo*, which means 'cat that looks like tree bark', because of the ring-shaped markings on their coats. Their fur is also 'ticked', meaning that each hair on the cat is covered in alternating light and dark stripes. This makes the tabby pattern appear blurry, and would have helped the original cats stay camouflaged in the woods.

Like their wild relatives, Sokokes are sharp-eyed and incredibly clever, but they also have a deep love of human company. A Sokoke will always be waiting at the door when you get home to greet you with a cheerful chirp.

Sokokes are excellent climbers. To keep these nimble cats happy, provide a cat tree or some spaced shelves so they can show off their leaping skills.

CAT STATS
Country: Kenya **Coat:** Short and glossy
Colours and patterns: Ticked brown tabby **Personality:** Intelligent, family-orientated, alert

CATS IN ANCIENT EGYPT

We don't know exactly when cats became domesticated, but the ancient Egyptians were almost certainly the first people to treat the cat as more than just a pest controller. Images of cats were painted on the walls of Egyptian temples, statues were carved in their honour and thousands of cats were laid to rest in sacred tombs. In ancient Egypt, cats weren't only creatures to be cared for – they were beings to be worshipped. It's no wonder cats decided to stick around …

CAT CULT

To get an idea of the importance of cats in ancient Egyptian culture, you just need to take a look at Egyptian gods. One of the most powerful was Sekhmet, the goddess of war, disease and medicine, who had the head of a lion. Another was Bastet, the goddess of the home, fertility and childbirth. Originally a fierce lion goddess, over time Bastet became a tamer figure, usually depicted as a domestic cat or as a woman with a cat's head.

Viewed as a protector of the home, Bastet became a mega-popular god, and this may be one reason why cats were so prized. Statues, figurines and jewellery were made in Bastet's feline image, and people made pilgrimages to the city of Bubastis to visit her opulent temple, which was home to hundreds of cats.

Another name for Bastet was Pasht. It's thought this might be where the word 'puss' comes from.

CAT MUMMIES

When a family cat died in ancient Egypt, its humans would shave their eyebrows off to show their grief. The cats of wealthy people were also mummified and buried in ornate, mini sarcophaguses fit for a pharaoh. Cats weren't sent off into the afterlife alone – many were buried with a mummified mouse snack.

In 2011, archaeologists discovered what is thought to be the world's oldest pet cemetery in Berenice, Egypt, which included the graves of 536 cats. Some of these cats were buried with decorative iron collars and beaded necklaces, suggesting they were much-loved pets.

CATS RULE!

Ancient Egyptian cats were celebrated as friends of the gods, but they were also loved for practical reasons. They kept their owners' homes and grain stores safe by hunting mice, rats and venomous snakes and, in return, were treated as part of the family. It's thought that most Egyptian homes had at least one cat, with tomb paintings showing cats sitting at the feet of their owners and being fed treats.

A moggie called Gli lived in the Hagia Sophia Mosque in Istanbul, Turkey, for 16 years. She became a popular symbol of the mosque and even met US President Barack Obama when he visited the building in 2009.

RUSSIAN BLUE
RUSSIA

DONSKOY
RUSSIA

TURKISH ANGORA
TURKEY

TURKISH VAN
TURKEY

TURKISH SHORTHAIR
TURKEY

Duchess, the elegant white cat in the Disney film 'The Aristocats', is a Turkish Angora.

KANAANI
ISRAEL AND THE PALESTINIAN TERRITORIES

ARABIAN MAU
UAE

SIBERIAN
RUSSIA

A Russian folktale tells the story of Bayun, a giant cat with a magical voice. Bayun's voice can cure any illness — but it can also lull people to sleep so Bayun can eat them for his supper!

KURILIAN BOBTAIL
RUSSIA

A group of Siberian cats were brought to live in the Hermitage Museum in St Petersburg during World War II to keep the museum's collections safe from rats and mice. Cats still patrol the museum today, though not all of them are Siberians.

WESTERN & NORTHERN ASIA
Domestic Breeds

Western and Northern Asia are home to some of the oldest and toughest kitties around. Many of these breeds have developed naturally to suit their environment (and their own rules) rather than being deliberately bred by humans. They include felines armed with thick coats to fend off fierce Russian winters, slinky shorthairs made for a life in hot deserts, and cats that think nothing of diving into a salty lake. If you're after a one-of-a-kind kitty, you've come to the right continent.

DOMESTIC CATS · WESTERN & NORTHERN ASIA

RUSSIAN BLUE

This distinguished cat comes from the remote Russian port of Archangel on the edge of the Arctic Circle. There, its handsome fur served a practical purpose – dense underneath and fine on top, it protected the cat from the bitterly cold climate. Russian blues were first brought to Europe by sailors in the 1800s, and their silvery-blue coat and dazzling green eyes quickly caught the attention of Victorian breeders. Since then, they have happily swapped ship life for sofas.

A Russian blue is a sensitive soul that expects you to run things in an orderly fashion, providing meals, playtime and cuddles according to schedule. Once you've won its trust, a Russian blue will reward you with infinite snuggles. Just as their ancestors might have scaled the rigging of a ship, these cats like to be up high and will gladly spend time perched on the shoulder of their favourite person.

- Large ears
- Long, slender legs
- Thick double coat
- Neat, round paws

CAT STATS
Country: Russia **Coat:** Short and thick
Colours and patterns: One colour – blue
Personality: Gentle, sensitive, intelligent

DONSKOY

Also known as the Don spyhnx, the Donskoy's story began in the city of Rostov-on-Don in Russia in 1987. A breeder rescued a stray kitten and was surprised when the cat's fur started to fall out. The cat later had kittens, some of which were born hairless, while others lost their hair as they grew up. Tests revealed that the cats carried a very strong gene that caused hairlessness. Not all cat associations recognise the Donskoy as a breed because of health concerns associated with this gene.

Because of their lack of fur, Donskoys should be kept as indoor cats. That suits these felines just fine as they love snuggling up to their humans like a smooth, purring hot-water bottle, but will appreciate a jumper when its chilly.

- Wedge-shaped head with large ears
- Almond-shaped eyes
- Thin, whip-like tail
- Usually has no hair or whiskers
- Firm body with wrinkled skin
- Webbed toes

CAT STATS
Country: Russia **Coat:** Four different coat types – 'rubber bald' (completely hairless), 'flocked' (a very fine layer of soft downy fur), 'velour' (a short coat and a bald spot on head), 'brush' (a short, bristly coat)
Colours and patterns: Various colours and patterns
Personality: Affectionate, inquisitive, active

SIBERIAN

Only the toughest kitties could survive in the freezing forests of Siberia in Northern Russia. With its waterproof coat, furry paws and sturdy body, the Siberian is built for whatever the weather can throw at it. The national cat of Russia, the Siberian was only officially recognised as a breed in the 1980s and 90s, but longhaired cats matching its description have existed in the country for centuries – the earliest-known record dates back to 1000 CE.

This intelligent and independent fluffball is deeply loyal to its owners and makes the ultimate cuddle buddy, welcoming you through the door with a deep, rumbling purr.

CAT STATS
Country: Russia **Coat:** Thick, double coat **Colours and patterns:** Various colours and patterns, including black, red and white, in solid, tabby and tortoiseshell **Personality:** Loyal, clever, affectionate

Tufted ears
Round, barrel-like body
Soft, fluffy coat that grows extra thick in winter
Bushy tail
Powerful back legs allow these cats to jump high
Fluffy paw pads to protect its feet from snow

Large round head
Alert expression
Slightly arched back
Short, kinked tail
Sturdy body
Back legs are longer than the front

KURILIAN BOBTAIL

This striking short-tailed breed comes from the Kuril Islands, an archipelago that lies between Japan and the Kamchatka Peninsula and Sakhalin Island on Russia's east coast. The cats developed naturally in these areas for at least 200 years before being brought to the Russian mainland in the 20th century. The shape of this breed's signature short tail is unique to each cat – it can bend in any direction and be firm or flexible.

Quick-footed and clever, Kurilian bobtails are prized in Russia for their mouse-catching skills and are also said to be fond of fishing due to their island-hopping origins. While Kurilian bobtails will strike fear into anything small or scaly, they are people-loving cats that usually form a particularly strong bond with one lucky person in their human family.

CAT STATS
Country: Russia **Coat:** Short or long **Colours and patterns:** Most colours and patterns, including red, grey and brown, tabby and tortoiseshell **Personality:** Adaptable, smart, playful

DOMESTIC CATS • WESTERN & NORTHERN ASIA

TURKISH VAN

In the far east of Turkey, surrounded by rocky mountains, lies Lake Van – the country's largest lake and the home of a very special cat. Sometimes called the 'Turkish swimming cat', the Turkish Van is a true water baby. Although not all cats hate water, the Turkish Van is unusual because it will leap into a stream without a second thought – some even join their owners in the bath!

The cat's swimming skills were perfected in the salty waters of Lake Van, and the breed developed naturally in the lakeside towns and countryside over hundreds of years. In the 1950s, two British women who were holidaying in the area fell in love with these quirky cats and decided to set up a breeding programme.

While a Turkish Van enjoys quick cuddles, it is not a cat that will keep its paws still or on solid ground for long – a Van adores climbing. If you welcome one of these acrobatic cats into your home, it won't be long before your Van is balancing on the tops of doors or shimmying along curtain rails.

CAT STATS
Country: Turkey **Coat:** Long, soft and silky
Colours and patterns: Vans have a white coat with coloured markings on head and tail. Vankedisis are solid white. **Personality:** Entertaining, active, intelligent

All Vans have a chalk-white coat and distinctive 'top and tail' markings. A pure white version of the breed is called a 'Vankedisi'.

- *Oval-shaped eyes with an alert expression*
- *Some Turkish Vans have one amber eye and one blue eye*
- *Lush, water-repellent fur*
- *Tufted paw pads*
- *Long, plumed tail*
- *Sturdy body*
- *Grows a thicker coat during winter*

TURKISH ANGORA

A national treasure in Turkey, the Turkish Angora is a very beautiful and very old breed. It takes its name from the country's capital, Ankara (which used to be called Angora). First recorded in Europe in the 1500s, Angoras were adored for their exquisitely soft fur, and they played a key role in creating the Persian breed (p40) in the 1800s.

Unfortunately, the Angora was overshadowed by the success of the Persian and had almost disappeared completely by the 20th century. Only a few cats remained in a zoo in Ankara, where a programme was set up to save the breed. Sweet-natured and spirited, these charming cats are still considered rare today.

CAT STATS
Country: Turkey **Coat:** Long, soft and silky
Colours and patterns: Traditional colour is white, but today, the breed comes in various other colours and patterns, including black, chocolate, tabby, smoke and tortoiseshell
Personality: Affectionate, athletic, refined

Fine, glossy coat · Large ears · Graceful body · Almond-shaped eyes with an alert expression · Small, round paws · Long, fluffy tail

TURKISH SHORTHAIR

Also known as the Anatolian, the Turkish shorthair has a similar build and personality to the Turkish Van (see opposite). However, while the Van has been refined and developed into a breed, the Turkish shorthair has a more unofficial status and not much is known about its history. You're more likely to bump into these cats on the streets of Istanbul than see them in a show ring.

Mellow and friendly, Turkish shorthairs enjoy being around people, but they are also practical souls and perfectly capable of looking after themselves. Like Turkish Vans, these cats enjoy playing with water and are not afraid of getting their paws wet.

Strong, medium-sized body · Broad head · Intelligent expression · Strong, round paws · Muscular legs

CAT STATS
Country: Turkey **Coat:** Short and thick
Colours and patterns: Any colour and pattern, including the classic white-and-red Van markings
Personality: Cheerful, calm, adaptable

DOMESTIC CATS • WESTERN & NORTHERN ASIA

Big ears

Elegant neck

Slender body

Large eyes

Triangular-shaped head

Long legs with neat paws

KANAANI

This rare and unusual breed was developed in Jerusalem in the 1990s and 2000s by a sculptor called Doris Pollatschek. She wanted to create a cat that looked like the African wildcats (p106) that prowl the deserts and scrublands of Africa and Central Asia, but with a home-loving personality. Bengals (p32), Abyssinians (p70) and Orientals (p72) as well as African wildcats were all added to the mix. The breed was refined over the years to create an elegant and gentle feline, which still has a dash of its wild ancestors' spirit.

A Kanaani is a beautiful creature but if you're after a calm, cuddly cat, you've come to the wrong page! These agile kitties love to run, jump and explore all sorts of high places, so they need a home with plenty of toys and playtime.

CAT STATS
Country: Israel and the Palestinian Territories
Coat: Short and coarse **Colours and patterns:** Various colours with spotted and marbled tabby patterns **Personality:** Active, calm, affectionate

ARABIAN MAU

The deserts of the Arabian Peninsula have been the kingdom of a very special cat for over 1,000 years. The Arabian mau developed naturally from felines that lived a tough (and hot!) existence among the sand dunes. Like their ancestors, today's Arabian maus have short fur without an undercoat and very large ears. Both features allow the cats to shed heat and keep cool under the fierce Arabian sun.

Arabian maus are resourceful and unfussy cats that are used to fending for themselves – many can still be found living a feral life in cities throughout the Middle East. When kept as pets, maus have a reputation for being outstandingly loyal to their humans and are said to be particularly devoted to children in their family.

Built for dashing across the desert or tiptoeing over rooftops, this is an outdoorsy and agile breed that is happiest with an equally active human playmate. Cat trees are a great way to keep an Arabian mau entertained, while interactive toys will let this cat show off its impressive hunting skills.

CAT STATS
Country: Kuwait, Qatar, Saudi Arabia and the United Arab Emirates **Coat:** Short **Colours and patterns:** Any colour and pattern, but often found in black, white and brown with tabby markings **Personality:** Athletic, smart, loyal

- Firm chin with well-defined whisker pads
- Large, wide ears
- Oval, slightly slanted, eyes
- Muscular body
- Long legs with neat, oval paws
- Long tail

HOW TO SPEAK CAT

If you haven't spent much time with cats before, they can seem like hard animals to read. Cats have a delicate way of expressing themselves, showing their feelings through small changes in their ears, eyes, tail and posture. Sometimes you need to look at all these features together to get the message. Learning how to read a cat's body language, and understanding when they're happy, want attention or need space, means you can have the best possible relationship with your feline friend.

DON'T LOOK INTO MY EYES!

Cats don't like being stared at. In kitty talk, if you look at one another straight in the face you want to start a fight (1). When two cats meet and want to let each other know they're not a threat, they will gently blink at one another instead (2).

If you're meeting a cat for the first time, try a slow blink and then look away – this is a great way to tell a cat that you're a friend. If in doubt, it is always best to let a cat come to you to say hi than you go to them. Ever noticed that cats make a beeline for the human in the room who's ignoring them? To a cat, this seemingly standoff-ish behaviour is totally charming!

1. Unblinking stare

2. Slow blinks

You may have noticed that cats often greet people they know by rubbing against their legs. Smell is important to cats and transferring scent is a way of marking territory or forming social bonds. By rubbing itself against your leg, a cat is saying, 'You're part of my family!'

A HAPPY CAT

A happy cat will send out laid-back vibes – their ears will be held naturally, their eyes will look gentle, possibly half-closed, and their body will be relaxed. Here are three contented poses to look out for:

1. **Walking towards you** with their ears in a normal position and their tail straight up, sometimes with a curl at the tip. Your cat is saying, 'Welcome home, friend!'

2. **Sitting (or lying down)** in a relaxed way, with their tail held loosely, mouth closed and eyes a normal shape, means they are feeling chilled out.

3. **Rolling on their back**. Your cat isn't necessarily asking for a tummy rub. They show you their tummy, a sensitive part of their body, to say, 'I trust you very much, human!'

A WORRIED CAT

Once you know what a happy cat looks like, it is easier to pick up on signs that a cat might be feeling stressed or anxious. Keep an eye out for:

1. **A slowly swishing tail.** This normally means that a cat is feeling unsure or anxious. For example, the cat might be watching you swing a toy around, but doesn't know you very well, so feels uncertain about joining in the game.

2. **Crouching low to the ground or hiding.** This is a sign that a cat is feeling nervous – their tail may be tucked close to them, their ears will be flatter than normal, and their eyes will look wide and tense. The cat is telling you, 'I need some space'.

AN ANGRY CAT

Cats make it quite clear when they're not happy about something. If you see a cat doing any of these things, leave them well alone!

1. **Thrashing their tail** from side to side or thumping it on the floor. This means a cat is annoyed. Perhaps they've had enough strokes and want a bit of alone time – whatever it is, they're telling you to stop.

2. **Puffing up their tail.** Their back is arched and spiky, and ears are flat against their head. The cat might be hissing as well. This cat is feeling threatened and is about to attack.

PURR-LEASED TO MEET YOU?

Cats use a range of sounds to express themselves. A hiss or growl makes it plain that a cat is not in a good mood, while squeaks and chirps usually signal excitement. It's important to look at your cat's body language at the same time as listening to its voice. For example, purrs normally suggest that a cat is feeling relaxed, but cats may also purr to soothe themselves if they're feeling stressed or ill.

Kittens meow to get their mum's attention but adult cats rarely meow at one another – only to their humans. This is probably because cats see us as caregivers. A cat will often meow to you as a sign of greeting or to let you know they're in the room and ready for something (did someone say 'dinner'?).

The li hua is another clever cat. Apparently, one was even taught to fetch the morning paper for its owner!

Burmese cats are slender and elegant, but owing to their heavy bones and dense muscles, they can feel heavier than they look! They are sometimes referred to as 'bricks wrapped in silk' because of their surprising heaviness.

According to legend, a pair of Siamese cats were asked to guard a precious golden goblet by the Buddha. They wrapped their tails tightly around the goblet to keep it safe and, as a result, their tails became bent. It used to be common for Siamese cats to have a slightly bent tail, but this trait has been bred out of most modern Siamese.

1. **LI HUA** CHINA
2. **SINGAPURA** SINGAPORE
3. **JAPANESE BOBTAIL** JAPAN
4. **KHAO MANEE** THAILAND
5. **KORAT** THAILAND
6. **SIAMESE** THAILAND
7. **ABYSSINIAN** SOUTHEAST ASIA
8. **MEKONG BOBTAIL** SOUTHEAST ASIA
9. **CEYLON** SRI LANKA
10. **BURMESE** MYANMAR
11. **AUSTRALIAN MIST** AUSTRALIA
12. **MANDALAY** NEW ZEALAND
13. **TEMPLECAT** NEW ZEALAND

The Abyssinian is one of the smartest breeds of cat in the world. These feline Einsteins can learn all kinds of tricks, from rolling over and high fiving to jumping through hoops.

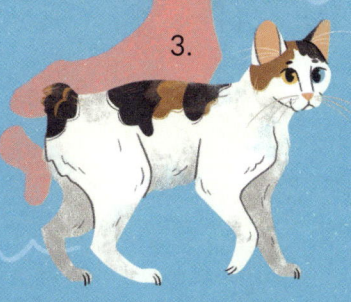

Cat cafes are places where customers can watch and play with cats. They are especially popular in Japan, where many rented homes and apartment buildings don't allow people to keep pets.

Southern, Southeast and East ASIA & AUSTRALASIA

Domestic Breeds

Welcome to the land of some truly fabulous felines. The ancestors of many Asian cats were originally bred to warm the laps of emperors and monks. Cherished inside palaces and temples, their beauty and character have remained unchanged for generations. Two in particular have become some of the most recognisable breeds in the world – the slinky Siamese and the beautiful Burmese. Australia and New Zealand's felines are newer kitties on the block, developed for a more practical, but no less-princely, life in modern homes.

DOMESTIC CATS · SOUTHERN, SOUTHEAST AND EAST ASIA & AUSTRALASIA

LI HUA

Also known as the dragon li in their home country, the li hua (you say it 'lee wah') is thought to have developed naturally from wild cats, rather than being created by crossing other breeds. Cats matching the description of the li hua have been keeping Chinese homes free of mice and slinking their way into art and folk stories for centuries. In one famous Chinese tale, a baby prince is stolen and replaced by a cat!

These sturdy tabbies are free-spirited and need room to roam. But despite their independent side, they have gentle and easy-going characters. A li hua will happily settle in a busy family and make a faithful friend in most homes.

CAT STATS
Country: China **Coat:** Short and thick **Colours and patterns:** Brown mackerel tabby **Personality:** Clever, loyal, active

Alert, pointed ears

Black markings at the corners of the mouth make these cats look like they're smiling.

Large almond-shaped eyes, typically green or yellow and brown

Glossy, tabby-patterned coat

Ring markings and a black tip on tail

Strong, rectangular body

SINGAPURA

The origins of these dainty cats are unclear, but it is thought they developed from a colony of street cats found in the small island country of Singapore in Southeast Asia, where they were known as 'river cats' or 'drain cats'. In the 1970s, a litter of kittens was taken to America where they may have been crossed with Burmese and Abyssinians to create this elegant breed.

Singapuras are the smallest breed of domestic cat, but what they lack in size they make up for with a big, bold personality. These active cats are especially fond of climbing – whether that's up furniture or your shoulders – and their huge, sparkly eyes reflect their mischievous characters.

CAT STATS
Country: Singapore **Coat:** Short and fine **Colours and patterns:** Only one colour called 'sepia agouti' – an ivory-coloured coat with dark-brown shades **Personality:** Playful, inquisitive, loving

Big ears

Very large gold-green eyes, with a black outline

Small build

Muscular body

Slender tail with a dark tip

JAPANESE BOBTAIL

Count yourself lucky if you're friends with a Japanese bobtail. In their home-country of Japan, these neat cats are thought to bring good fortune to a household, especially the tortoiseshell and white variety, known as the *mi-ke* (three colour).

All Japanese bobtails are born with a naturally short, curly tail, which is covered in fluffy fur, giving it a pom-pom-like look. They are intelligent, outgoing felines that like to be part of the action, and are perfectly capable of learning tricks or walking on a lead if you put in the time. Bobtails are chatty too, using a range of sweet little chirps and sing-song meows to talk to their owners.

Although bobtails have been prized pets in Japanese homes for hundreds of years, they weren't widely known elsewhere till the 1960s, when a group of cats were taken to the United States to start a breeding programme. Today, both the shorthaired and longhaired varieties bring love (and luck) to families around the world.

CAT STATS
Country: Japan **Coat:** Short or longhaired, soft and silky with no undercoat **Colours and patterns:** Most colours; white and tortoiseshell is especially sought after **Personality:** Busy, affectionate, smart

Curly, pom-pom tail

Gently curved, triangular head

Wide, expressive ears

Large, oval eyes

Slender, muscly body

Back legs are slightly longer than front legs

The traditional 'maneki-neko' (beckoning cat) figurines, common throughout Japan and thought to bring good luck, depict a welcoming bobtail cat.

DOMESTIC CATS · SOUTHERN, SOUTHEAST AND EAST ASIA & AUSTRALASIA

KHAO MANEE

The khao manee (you say it 'cow man-ee') is the feline jewel in the Thai royal crown. *Khao manee* means 'white gem' in Thai, and for hundreds of years these sparkly eyed cats were only allowed to be owned and bred by members of the Thai royal family. Living a life of luxury in opulent palaces, the cats weren't seen outside of Thailand until the late 1990s when a US breeder introduced several to America.

Because they spent so much of their history playing with princes and princesses, khao manees adore being around people. Confident and talkative, these cats enjoy greeting visitors to their kingdoms and graciously accept fuss from their human subjects with a chorus of purrs and chirrups.

Heart-shaped head
Jewel-like eyes; odd-coloured eyes are particularly sought after
Pink nose
Shiny white coat
Pink paw pads

CAT STATS
Country: Thailand **Coat:** Short and fine
Colours and patterns: One colour – white
Personality: Confident, chatty, curious

The khao manee is an ancient breed. These cats feature in a book of cat poems called the 'Tamra Maew' printed in Thailand in 1350. The poems describe the cats as being 'white as crystal' and with eyes 'like diamonds'.

Large, round green eyes
Heart-shaped face
Muscular body
Neat, oval paws

KORAT

If the khao manee (see above) is Thailand's gem, then the korat is the country's lucky charm. Considered a symbol of good fortune for hundreds of years, korats were traditionally gifted in pairs to Thai couples on their wedding day to bring luck and health to a marriage. These special cats were introduced to the rest of the world in 1959, when a pair was sent to the USA to start a breeding programme.

The korat's distinctive features are its rich, silver-blue coat and bright green eyes. An ancient book of cat poems, the *Tamra Maew*, describes the breed's eyes as 'like dew when dropped on the leaf of a lotus'.

CAT STATS
Country: Thailand **Coat:** Short, thick and silky
Colours and patterns: Silver-blue **Personality:** Intelligent, loyal, loving

Large ears

Blue, almond-shaped eyes

Wedge-shaped head with a long nose

Long, slender body

Slim legs

Dainty paws

SIAMESE

This slinky breed is named after Siam, the old name for Thailand. Although its exact origins are a bit of a mystery, it is thought that it dates back to the 14th century, when it was first mentioned in a Thai manuscript. What is certain is that ever since its arrival in Europe in the 1870s, the Siamese has become one of the world's most recognisable and beloved breeds.

Siamese cats have notoriously strong personalities and voices to match their stunning looks. These cats have a particularly loud meow (nicknamed a 'meezer') and are not shy about making their feelings heard. As well as being noisy, they are also nosy. An extremely intelligent feline, Siamese enjoy opening cabinets, watching TV and finding the best lookout spots in their homes (they love to climb).

When they're not exploring, Siamese will stick by their favourite person's side like elegant, chatty shadows. These cats love attention and can become unhappy if left alone. Many people adopt Siamese in pairs, so their cats always have company. It's a demanding breed, but this enchanting and entertaining cat is worth every bit of effort.

CAT STATS
Country: Thailand **Coat:** Short, fine and glossy
Colours and patterns: All Siamese have pointed markings (a pale body with a darker tail, paws and ears). The colours include seal, blue, lilac, red, cream, tabby, tortoiseshell **Personality:** Intelligent, talkative, outgoing

DOMESTIC CATS • SOUTHERN, SOUTHEAST AND EAST ASIA & AUSTRALASIA

ABYSSINIAN

The Abyssinian is a captivating cat with an intriguing history. The breed was named after Abyssinia (now Ethiopia) in Africa and developed in the UK from the 1890s onwards. It was once thought that these graceful felines were descended from ancient Egyptian cats, but DNA tests showed that their ancestors actually came from the coast of Southeast Asia.

With a rich golden coat and athletic body, the Abyssinian wouldn't look out of place prowling through an Asian jungle. These stealthy cats love to be kept busy learning tricks (they're great at fetch), playing with puzzle toys or leaping up climbing frames. They build deep bonds with their owners but these intelligent cats will generally do what they please … and expect you to keep up!

A longhaired version of the Abyssinian, called the Somali (p20), was developed in the USA in the 1950s.

Alert ears
Large eyes
Wedge-shaped head
Long, lean body
Elegant legs with dainty paws

CAT STATS
Country: Originated in Southeast Asia and developed as a breed in the UK **Coat:** Short, fine and dense **Colours and patterns:** Traditional coat colour is agouti – tawny-coloured fur with dark tips; other colours include blue, fawn, chocolate and silver **Personality:** Inquisitive, loyal, energetic

Large blue eyes
Rectangular body
Short, kinked tail
Strong back legs which are longer than front legs

MEKONG BOBTAIL

No, it's not a Siamese that's lost its tail – it's a Mekong bobtail! These pretty cats developed naturally in Southeast Asia and are named after the mighty Mekong River that flows through the region. They weren't known in the rest of the world until the 19th century, when the king of Thailand gave several bobtails to the Russian emperor.

Like other short-tailed breeds, the Mekong bobtail is a bouncy little soul. They love to use their nimble paws to jump and climb, but also enjoy snuggling with their family when they've worn themselves out.

CAT STATS
Country: Various countries across Southeast Asia, including Thailand, Vietnam and China **Coat:** Short and glossy **Colours and patterns:** Any colour in a pointed pattern (pale body with darker ears, legs and tail) **Personality:** Active, playful, friendly

CEYLON

These very rare cats with golden coats and dainty tabby markings come from the island nation of Sri Lanka (which used to be called Ceylon). They probably developed naturally there for centuries, cut off from cat populations on the mainland. In the 1980s, the cats caught the attention of a visiting Italian vet, who decided to take several back to Italy to start a breeding programme.

They are still an uncommon breed, but those who have been lucky enough to meet a Ceylon describe them as sweet-natured and gentle – and, true to their tropical roots, partial to a coconut snack! Like all tabby cats, Ceylons have an M-shaped marking on the top of their head. Some have an extra diamond-shaped marking called a 'cobra', which is considered particularly special in their home country.

> **CAT STATS**
> **Country:** Sri Lanka **Coat:** Short and fine **Colours and patterns:** Traditional colour is manila (sandy fur with black tips); other colours include blue, red and cream with tabby markings **Personality:** Friendly, calm, playful

Wide ears • Large eyes with dark rims • Faint tabby markings on head, neck and legs • Muscular legs • Elegant build

BURMESE

The modern Burmese developed out of various breeding programmes in the UK and USA during the 1930s–50s. But the origins of these charming cats go back much further. According to legend, they were the treasured pets of Buddhist monks in ancient Burma (now called Myanmar) and would have sauntered freely through temples and monasteries.

Today's Burmese expect to rule their homes (and people) in a similar way. A Burmese loves to share every moment of the day with its beloved owner, from supervising mealtimes to wriggling under the duvet with you at night. It's a chatty cat, but any demands are made in a soft, polite voice that is hard to say no to.

Round head • Large yellow eyes with a sweet expression • Fur has a soft, satin-like texture • Elegant yet robust body • Slim legs with neat paws

> **CAT STATS**
> **Country:** Myanmar **Coat:** Short and glossy **Colours and patterns:** Traditional colour is brown, but they also come in blue, lilac, red, cream, and tortoiseshell patterns **Personality:** Clever, playful, loving

ORIENTAL CATS

The ancestors of all cats in the Oriental group originally came from Thailand, but the group was developed in the UK and USA from the 1950s onwards by crossing Siamese cats (p69) with various other breeds. Orientals come in a kaleidoscope of 300 kitty colours and patterns, from solid, shaded and bicolour to tabby, tortoiseshell and smoke. These cats are charming, chatty and adore being close to their people. Let's meet some!

1 ORIENTAL TORTOISESHELL

Breeders started to experiment with Oriental tortoiseshells in the 1960s by crossing single-coloured Orientals with red- and tortoiseshell-point Siamese. Tortoiseshell cats are almost always female. Like the rest of the Oriental group, these colourful cats are bold and people-loving. Whatever it is you're doing, this cat will want to lend a paw!

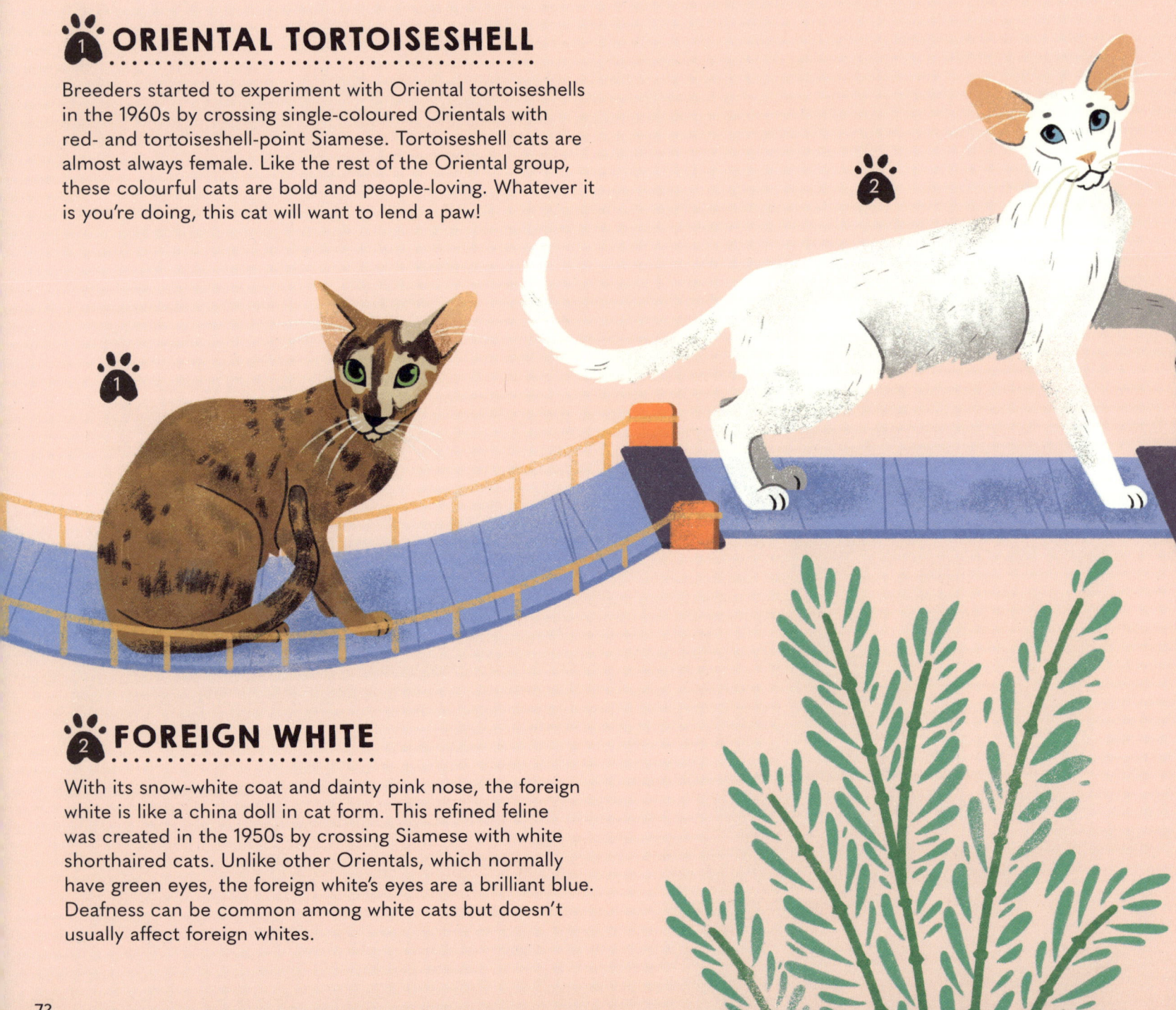

2 FOREIGN WHITE

With its snow-white coat and dainty pink nose, the foreign white is like a china doll in cat form. This refined feline was created in the 1950s by crossing Siamese with white shorthaired cats. Unlike other Orientals, which normally have green eyes, the foreign white's eyes are a brilliant blue. Deafness can be common among white cats but doesn't usually affect foreign whites.

ORIENTAL SHADED

Shaded Oriental cats have tabby coats, but the markings only feature at the very tips of the fur, giving the pattern a faded appearance. This super-stylish branch of the Oriental family tree was created in the 1970s, when a Siamese bred with a silver-coated (or 'Chinchilla') Persian (p40). Kittens can have strong tabby markings but these get lighter as the cats get older.

ORIENTAL TABBY

Single-colour Oriental cats were proving so popular by the 1970s that breeders turned their attention to creating tabby versions. Nowadays, Oriental cats can be found in all tabby colours, with classic, ticked, mackerel or spotted markings. Like other Orientals, these athletic cats have kittenish personalities, and enjoy being kept on their toes with games of fetch, agility and chaser toys.

ORIENTAL LONGHAIR

This stunning cat was developed in the 1960s by crossing Siamese cats with Abyssinians (p70) that carried a longhaired gene. Despite its glamorous looks, don't expect an Oriental longhair to sit around all day looking pretty – this mischievous cat likes to be the life and soul of the party.

ASIAN CATS

Although they were developed in the UK and USA, all cats in the Asian group can trace their roots back to the Burmese (p71). Sometimes called 'Burmese in fancy pyjamas', these cats are essentially Burmese with different-coloured coats and they feature a dash of another breed in their ancestry. Outgoing and people-loving like their Burmese grandparents, these beautiful cats make dignified and loving companions.

BOMBAY

There are two versions of this all-black Burmese: the American Bombay (created in the USA in 1950s by crossing a Burmese with an American shorthair) and the British Bombay (developed in the 1980s by crossing a Burmese with a black domestic shorthaired cat). Both types are named after the Indian city of Bombay (now called Mumbai) as a nod to the cat's resemblance to the Indian black leopard. As well as their jet-black fur and large golden eyes, Bombay cats have a distinctive swagger when they walk – just like a mini panther!

ASIAN TABBY

The Asian tabby appears in all tabby patterns – classic, mackerel, spotted and ticked – and a huge range of colours, from black, chocolate and red to cream, caramel and silver. Like other Asian cats, they are playful and peace-loving. Asians enjoy human company most of all and like to be in a household where they are given lots of attention.

4 TIFFANIE

The Tiffanie (also known as the Burmilla longhair) is the only member of the Asian group to inherit its Persian ancestor's long, glossy locks. In all other respects, it is identical to other Asian cats and comes in the same colours and patterns. Sensitive souls, Tiffanies prefer a quiet home with gentle play and lots of cuddles.

3 BURMILLA

The Burmilla is where it all began. The first breed to belong to the Asian group, it was developed in the UK in the 1980s after a Burmese accidentally bred with a Chinchilla Persian. Their kittens inherited their Persian dad's stunning silver-tipped coat, and were so pretty that their owner decided to create a new breed. Combining the calm character of the Persian and the inquisitive nature of the Burmese, Burmillas are sweet-natured as well as showstopping felines.

5 ASIAN SMOKE

After the popularity of the Burmilla, breeders started experimenting with other Burmese variations. The smoke is one example. Cats with 'smoke' coats have double-coloured fur – the root of each hair on the cat is pale but the tip of the hair is coloured. This is usually only noticeable when the cat moves or the fur is parted, and creates an elegant, cloudy effect.

DOMESTIC CATS • SOUTHERN, SOUTHEAST AND EAST ASIA & AUSTRALASIA

AUSTRALIAN MIST

The only cat breed to come from Australia, this easy-going and friendly feline reflects the sunny spirit of its home country. The Australian mist was first created in the 1970s by crossing Burmese (p71), Abyssinians (p70) and domestic shorthaired cats.

Many areas of Australia have rules about allowing cats to roam outside because of the harm they can cause to native wildlife, so the Australian mist was created to live as an indoor-only cat. That suits these home-loving felines just fine. While Australian mists are playful as kittens, they grow into calm adults that much prefer cuddles than doing anything too energetic.

Australian mists are always keen to lend a paw around the house, supervising you while you make the bed or unpack the food shopping. They have been known to open fridges to help themselves to a snack when their owners aren't looking! These even-tempered souls will fill a home with contented purrs and make excellent companions for families as well as older people.

Australian mists have a ticked, or agouti, coat, which means each hair on the cat is striped in light and dark colours. This makes the tabby pattern on the cat appear faded, or 'misty'.

CAT STATS
Country: Australia **Coat:** Short **Colours and patterns:** Brown, blue, lilac, chocolate, gold or peach, with spotted or marbled ticked tabby pattern **Personality:** Laid-back, loving, gentle

Large ears with rounded tips

Green eyes with a gentle expression

Muscular body

Short, sleek fur

Long, thick tail

Large golden eyes
Round head
Short coat, which is silkier than the Burmese's
Firm, muscular body
Slender legs with oval paws

MANDALAY

This sleek kitty was developed in New Zealand in the 1970s and 1980s when Burmese (p71) were crossed with local moggies. The resulting kittens had bewitching gold eyes like their Burmese parents and very dark, rich coats.

Mandalays are similar to Burmese in looks and personality – just more intense! They are strong-minded cats that enjoy attention and spending time in the company of their favourite human. Whether they're snuggling on your shoulder while you watch TV or stealing your socks, Mandalays are some of the most elegant and fun felines around.

CAT STATS
Country: New Zealand **Coat:** Short and very glossy **Colours and patterns:** Various colours, including black, chocolate, cinnamon and cream **Personality:** Clever, affectionate, outgoing

TEMPLECAT

Do you like the Birman (p46)? Then you'll love the templecat! This new feline was dreamt up in the 2000s by a New Zealand breeder who wanted a cat with the looks and sweet nature of the Birman but with a shorter, more easy-to-care-for coat.

The templecat is a very rare breed, but it is quickly winning over hearts in New Zealand. Gentle like the Birman but with a more outgoing personality, this stunning cat greets everyone it meets with a cheerful, soft purr and makes a wonderful, cuddly companion.

CAT STATS
Country: New Zealand **Coat:** Short and silky **Colours and patterns:** Pointed coat in seal, blue, chocolate, lilac, red, cream, cinnamon and fawn colours **Personality:** Gentle, affectionate, intelligent

The name 'templecat' was chosen to reflect the breed's Birman ancestry. Birmans are descended from cats that lived in ancient temples in Myanmar (which used to be called Burma).

Big blue eyes
Silky coat with a springy texture
Long, thick tail
Large paws with white 'sock' markings
Long, sturdy body

NATURAL INSTINCTS

Domestic cats share many behaviours with their wild relatives – this is part of what makes cats so fascinating and fun to be around. Here are some common instincts you might have spotted, and some ways your cat can satisfy them at home.

SLEEPING

Cats are the ultimate nappers. On average, domestic cats sleep for 12–18 hours a day, usually during daylight hours. Cats sleep so much so that, when they are awake, they have lots of energy to hunt, patrol and protect their territory. Although a pet cat doesn't need to worry about these things, it will still sleep a lot so it has energy for playing and exploring. Cats are most active at dawn, dusk and night, so it is perfectly normal for a cat to be scampering around your house after lights out!

HUNTING

As cuddly as they are, even the laziest kitty is capable of being a hunter when the mood strikes – that's just the way cats are made. Cats are carnivores (meat-eaters) and have an overwhelming instinct to hunt anything small, squeaky and fast-moving. Keep your cat indoors at dawn and dusk – when cats are most hard-wired to hunt and when wild animals are most active. It's also important to play chase and pouncing games with your cat so it can burn off energy and to act on its hunting instincts in a safe way.

CLIMBING

Like wild cats, domestic cats enjoy being high up, especially when they want to have a snooze. Scampering to the top of a cupboard allows a cat to get a good look at their territory and makes them feel safe, as they can spot any danger coming their way (like an over-excitable dog). Providing a cat with a cat tower to climb, play and sleep on means they can test their head for heights in a safe, kitty-friendly way.

You can get quick-release cat collars, which you can attach a bell to. This will alert small creatures when your cat approaches, but will unclip if your cat gets its collar caught in something, keeping both local wildlife and your kitty safe.

SCRATCHING

Wild cats scratch tall, sturdy objects such as tree trunks for two reasons – to keep their claws sharp and a good length and to let other cats in the neighbourhood know they are there (and this tree belongs to them!). This is exactly what your cat is doing when it scratches your sofa. To keep your cat happy and protect your furniture, give your cat a scratching post or mat to use instead.

Introduction to WILD CATS

So far, we have focused on one species of cat, the domestic cat (*Felis catus*). But there's a whole wide world of cats out there! In this half of the book, we'll meet 40 wild cat species that prowl the planet today. From the mighty tiger and the speedy cheetah to the acrobatic margay and stilt-legged serval, each species has developed unique skills and incredible adaptations to help it thrive in its natural habitat.

BIG CAT OR SMALL CAT?

Wild cats can be split into two main groups – the big cats (Pantherinae) and the small cats (Felinae). Lions (1), tigers, jaguars, leopards, snow leopards and clouded leopards are all members of the 'big cat' group. The small cat group includes medium-sized species, such as the ocelot (2), caracal and Canada lynx, as well as little felines, such as the sand cat (3) and rusty-spotted cat. They may be less well-known than their larger cousins, but small wild cats lead equally fascinating and remarkable lives. Cheetahs and pumas, although large in size, are usually grouped with small cats because they lack a key big-cat feature – they can't roar.

An easy way to remember the difference between the two groups is that big cats roar and small cats purr. However, only four members of the big cat group – the lion, tiger, jaguar and leopard – actually roar. They can do this thanks to the special structure of their vocal cords. Although snow leopards and clouded leopards can't roar, they are still classed as big cats because they share similar physical characteristics with other members of the group.

WHERE DO WILD CATS LIVE?

Wild cats are found throughout Europe, Asia, Africa and North and South America. A large number of wild cat species live in woodland or rainforests, but they also inhabit an amazing range of environments across the globe – from mountains and deserts to swamps and grasslands. Many are experts at stalking prey on the ground, while others trip through the trees to catch a meal or leap into the air to snare birds. Some even dive into rivers to catch fish!

ENDANGERED CATS

Wild cats are some of the most iconic animals on the planet. It's hard to imagine Africa's savanna without lions or India's forests without tigers. Despite this, most of the world's wild cat species are threatened in some way by the actions of humans. You can find out more about the challenges wild cats face throughout this section. The official conservation status of each species, which records whether the animal is at risk in its natural habitat, is noted in its 'Cat Stats' box.

Native to Spain and Portugal, the Iberian lynx is one of the world's most endangered species of cat. There are around 1,100 in the wild today.

NORTH & SOUTH AMERICA
Wild Cats

North and South America's incredible range of habitats – from icy tundra and hot deserts to lush rainforests and windswept canyons – supports a wide variety of wild cats. Some, like the Canada lynx and Andean cat, have evolved to be specialists in a particular environment. Others, like the puma and ocelot, call lots of different habitats home, crossing continents and prowling forests, plains and mountains. From some of the mightiest cats on the planet to the smallest and most secretive, welcome to the world of America's wild felines.

Margays are cunning cats that have been recorded imitating the calls of monkeys in order to catch them. They also hunt other small mammals, birds and reptiles.

A Canada lynx's paws are around 10 cm (3.9 in) wide – that's about as big as a bagel!

Jaguars have the most powerful bite of all the big cats. Their teeth are strong enough to pierce the tough skin of a caiman and crush a turtle's shell.

82

Eleven per cent of jaguars are 'melanistic', which means they have dark fur instead of gold. Although they appear to be all black, if you look closely at their coats, you'll see they have spotted markings, too.

The Andean cat's favourite food is the vizcacha, a type of rodent related to chinchillas, which makes up around 93 per cent of the cat's diet.

Pampas cats in colder regions have thick, dense coats, while those in hotter climates have thinner fur that's straw-like in texture.

1. CANADA LYNX
2. BOBCAT
3. PUMA
4. JAGUAR
5. MARGAY
6. OCELOT
7. ANDEAN CAT
8. GEOFFROY'S CAT
9. JAGUARUNDI
10. PAMPAS CAT
11. NORTHERN AND SOUTHERN TIGER CATS
12. KODKOD

83

WILD CATS · NORTH & SOUTH AMERICA

CANADA LYNX

The deep pine forests of Canada and Alaska are the lands of the lynx. Small populations also exist in some US states, including Maine, Montana, Colorado and Washington. This secretive cat spends most of its time alone, usually emerging from its den at twilight or night to hunt.

With its tufty ears and fluffy face, a Canada lynx may look cuddly, but it is a tough hunter that's built for life in a cold climate. Lynx grow thick coats in winter, and have long, powerful legs and large paws with furry pads. These features protect the cat from the cold and allow it to move easily across dense snow in search of a meal. Lynx use their large ears and excellent eyesight to find prey – they can spot a tiny mouse moving from 75 metres (250 feet) away.

Once it's found a target, a lynx will wait patiently for the perfect moment to pounce, sometimes for hours!

- Thick, grey coat in winter; thinner brown coat in summer
- Short tail with black tip
- Large, tufty ears with black tips
- Big eyes and ears help the lynx track prey at night
- Beard-like fur on face
- Round, small feet
- Very wide, webbed, furry paws, which act like snowshoes
- Long legs – back legs are longer than front legs to give them extra pouncing power

CAT STATS
Scientific name: *Lynx canadensis* **Habitat:** Boreal forests in North America **Weight:** 8–11 kg (18–24 lbs) **Length:** 73–106 cm (20–42 in) long plus a 10–15-cm (4–6-in) tail **Conservation status:** Least concern

BOBCAT

The bobcat is a close relative of the Canada lynx. It is smaller and redder than its silvery cousin, but has a similar build, with long legs, tufty ears and a stumpy, or 'bobbed', tail, which gives it its name.

Unlike the Canada lynx, bobcats are adaptable creatures that can make themselves at home in a desert, swamp or forest. The most common wild cat in North America, their unfussiness is the key to their success. A bobcat will eat practically anything it can get its paws on – from rabbits and rodents to snake eggs and fish. In 2015, a brave bobcat was even spotted pulling a small shark from the sea!

- Soft, dense fur with spotted or barred pattern for camouflage
- Ears with small tufts
- Short tail, but longer than that of the Canada lynx
- Straight back
- Black marking on the tip of the tail with white underneath
- Muscular legs
- Powerful paws, noticeably smaller than those of the Canada lynx

CAT STATS
Scientific name: *Lynx rufus* **Habitat:** Includes forests, swamps, deserts and scrubland. Found throughout North America, from southern Canada to Mexico **Weight:** 7–15 kg (15–33 lbs) **Length:** 50–120 cm (20–47 in) plus a 9–25-cm (4–10-in) tail **Conservation status:** Least concern

PUMA

Also known as the cougar, mountain lion or catamount, the puma is found across the Americas. Apart from humans, this resourceful cat has the greatest range of any land mammal in the Western hemisphere, proving just as happy in Canadian forests as in Arizona's desert canyons and South America's Andes Mountains.

Although the puma is the fourth-largest cat in the world (after tigers, lions and jaguars), it is classed as a small cat because it can't roar – instead it purrs. That might make it sound sweet, but you wouldn't want to mess with one. Pumas in North and Central America hunt deer, as well as smaller prey such as rodents and birds, while pumas in South America feed on llamas. These cats like to hunt during dawn and dusk, ambushing their prey from behind with a deadly bite.

For a large cat, pumas are surprisingly agile. Their powerful back legs allow them to leap around 12–13 metres (40–43 feet) in a single jump. And while they don't normally like to get their paws wet, pumas have been known to swim. In 2023, a male was spotted paddling more than a kilometre (almost a mile) across an estuary in north-west America.

> **CAT STATS**
> **Scientific name:** *Puma concolor* **Habitat:** Range of habitats, including forests, scrub, mountains and deserts across North, Central and South America **Weight:** 30–80 kg (66–176 lbs) **Length:** 200–250 cm (78–96 in) plus a 60–90-cm (24–35-in) tail **Conservation status:** Least concern

Long tail helps it balance when jumping or climbing

Short, tan-coloured fur

Black markings on tips of tail, ears and face

Tail lies close to the ground when the puma is walking

Strong back legs that allow it to jump great distances

A puma is born with spotty fur, which helps to camouflage it from predators. These markings have faded by the time the cub is around 9 months old and more independent.

WILD CATS · NORTH & SOUTH AMERICA

Thick tail

Orange-gold or black coats with open spotted markings called 'rosettes'

Large round head, sharp teeth and powerful jaws.

Large, flexible feet and big paws

The pattern on a jaguar's coat is similar to a leopard's (p105), but more complex. If you're not sure which cat you're looking at, search for a spot or two in the middle of the cat's rosettes – only jaguars have those.

JAGUAR

The rainforests of South America echo with the roar of the continent's largest cat – the jaguar. Its name comes from a word in the indigenous Tupí-Guaraní language, *yaguar*, which means 'he who kills in one leap'. It's no surprise that this awe-inspiring cat has been worshipped as a god by people in Central and South America since ancient times.

A fearsome hunter, the jaguar spends its nights (and sometimes part of the day) stalking the forests in search of large mammals such as tapir and capybara. Once a jaguar has found a target, it will wait silently in the shadows before pouncing, piercing the animal's skull with a single bite. Jaguars are also excellent swimmers and will readily pluck dangerous caiman from the water – or help themselves to caiman eggs if they fancy a snack.

As a cat that is most at home in the deep jungle, jaguars are severely threatened by deforestation. Since the 1880s, they have lost more than half of their territory. Much of the forest that remains has been broken up into fragments, trapping these mighty cats in small areas and making it hard for them to travel to find mates and food.

CAT STATS

Scientific name: *Panthera onca* **Habitat:** Forests, swamps, savanna and shrubland in Central and South America **Weight:** 36–148 kg (79–326 lbs) **Length:** 150–180 cm (60–72 in) plus a 68–90-cm (27–36-in) tail **Conservation status:** Near threatened

MARGAY

Like its larger cousin, the ocelot (see below), the margay is most active under cover of darkness. It likes to keep its paws off the ground, spending most of its time climbing, hunting or resting in trees. With huge eyes to help it see in the dark, the ability to leap over 2 metres (8 feet) in the air, and a long tail for balance, this acrobatic cat is perfectly adapted to a nocturnal life tiptoeing through the forest canopy.

The margay's secret weapons are its especially large, flexible feet, which help the cat to scamper across the thinnest of branches. If a margay ever slips, it can catch a branch in its big paws as it falls and stop itself from tumbling to the ground. Margays have even been known to hang upside-down from trees by their back legs to catch a hard-to-reach meal!

Long, heavy tail which acts as a counterweight to the cat's body as it climbs

Rounded ears

Longer face than ocelot

Beige-coloured coat, with a pattern of spots, stripes and blotches for camouflage

Huge, round eyes

CAT STATS
Scientific name: *Leopardus wiedii* **Habitat:** Various forest habitats, including tropical evergreen forests, deciduous forests and cloud forests in North and South America **Weight:** 2.3–4.9 kg (5–11 lbs) **Length:** 46–69 cm (18–27 in) plus a 23–52-cm (9–20-in) tail **Conservation status:** Near threatened

OCELOT

When the stars appear over the forests and grasslands of Central and South America, this sleek cat comes out to play. Ocelots are most active at night, when they use their big eyes and sharp hearing to detect prey. Mice, iguanas, monkeys or birds are all on the menu for an ocelot – they are not fussy eaters! About twice the size of a household cat, ocelots are brilliant climbers and are also happy to swim in order to catch fish and frogs.

An ocelot's soft, golden fur is peppered with spots, which are small on the cat's head and legs and form large, open bands on the cat's body. This dappled coat helps the ocelot blend in with its forest surroundings as it hunts, and also keeps it hidden while it rests during the day.

Short, smooth fur

Spotted coat keeps the cat camouflaged in the forest

Thick tail that's shorter than the margay's (see above)

Rounded ears

Stripes on cheeks and around neck

Ocelots have small litters made up of one to three kittens. The kittens are born with blue eyes and grey fur, which turns gold when they're a few months old.

CAT STATS
Scientific name: *Leopardus pardalis* **Habitat:** Rainforests, swamps, shrubland and savannas in Central and South America and in southwestern United States **Weight:** 11–16 kg (24–35 lbs) **Length:** 50–101 cm (20–40 in) plus a 30–50-cm (12–20-in) tail **Conservation status:** Least concern, but numbers are declining

WILD CATS · NORTH & SOUTH AMERICA

ANDEAN CAT

Known as 'the ghost of the Andes', this rarely seen cat lives in some of the remotest parts of South America's Andes Mountains. It is a mountaineering pro, with big paws for climbing, a thick coat to keep out the cold, and grey-brown markings to help it blend in against the rocks as it hunts. With an estimated 1,400 adult Andean cats left in the wild, it is the most endangered cat species in the Americas.

CAT STATS
Scientific name: *Leopardus jacobitus* **Habitat:** Mountain regions in Peru, Bolivia, Chile and Argentina. Sometimes steppe and scrub habitats **Weight:** 4–6 kg (9–13 lbs) **Length:** 57–75 cm (22–30 in) plus a 41–48-cm (16–19-in) tail **Conservation status:** Endangered

GEOFFROY'S CAT

Named after a 19th-century French naturalist, this adaptable feline makes its home in a wide range of habitats in South America. Although it is an agile climber, the Geoffroy's cat prefers to stay on the ground, using dense forests and grasslands for cover and camouflage. If it does need to have a look around, this little cat perches on its back legs like a meerkat. It is not picky about what it hunts, with rodents, small birds, fish, lizards and frogs all forming part of its diet.

CAT STATS
Scientific name: *Leopardus geoffroyi* **Habitat:** Pampas grassland, marshes, forests, shrublands, semi-desert and steppe in Bolivia, Brazil, Paraguay, Argentina, Uruguay and Chile **Weight:** 2–6 kg (4–13 lbs) **Length:** 43–88 cm (17–34 in) plus a 23–40-cm (9–16-in) tail **Conservation status:** Least concern

JAGUARUNDI

This is not an otter that's snuck into this book by mistake. This strange-looking feline is the jaguarundi and it is unlike any other small cat in South America. The species is thought to have evolved from cats that travelled from Asia to the Americas via a land bridge thousands of years ago, meaning jaguarundis are more closely related to pumas (p85) and cheetahs (p105) than their American neighbours. Jaguarundis are good climbers and swimmers and make an unusually wide range of noises for a cat – at least 13 different calls have been recorded, including purrs, whistles, chirps and yaps.

CAT STATS
Scientific name: *Herpailurus yagouaroundi* **Habitat:** Grassland, swamps, savanna and forests in Central and South America **Weight:** 4.5–9 kg (10–20 lbs) **Length:** 90–130 cm (35–51 in) plus a 30–60-cm (12–24-in) tail **Conservation status:** Least concern

PAMPAS CAT

This little cat is named after the pampas, an area of large grassy plains in South America, but it is equally at home in forests, swamps and parts of the Andes Mountains. Normally about the size of a chunky domestic tabby, its coat colour ranges from grey to reddish-brown. Its main source of food is thought to be small mammals, such as guinea pigs and mice, but this feisty feline has been known to take on flamingos and occasionally goats.

CAT STATS
Scientific name: *Leopardus colocolo* **Habitat:** Grassland, cloud forests, scrublands, savanna, swamps and woodlands across South America **Weight:** 3–4 kg (6.6–9 lbs) **Length:** 42–79 cm (16.5–31 in) plus a 22-33-cm (9–13-in) tail **Conservation status:** Near threatened

NORTHERN AND SOUTHERN TIGER CATS

These graceful felines are some of the smallest wild cats in South America. The northern tiger cat ranges from Costa Rica to Brazil, while the southern tiger cat is found in Brazil, Paraguay and north-eastern Argentina. Usually active at twilight or night, tiger cats stalk small rodents, birds and tree frogs. The blotchy markings on their coat help them blend in with the dappled sunlight on the forest floor if they do venture out in the daytime.

CAT STATS
Scientific name: *Leopardus tigrinus* (northern), *Leopardus guttulus* (southern) **Habitat:** Forests, scrubland and savanna (northern), rainforests, woodland, savanna and beaches (southern) **Weight:** 1.8–3.5 kg (4–8 lbs) **Length:** 38–59 cm (15–23 in) plus a 20-42-cm (8–16-in) tail **Conservation status:** Vulnerable

KODKOD

Meet the kodkod – the smallest wild cat in the Americas. About half the size of a domestic cat, it makes its home in mossy forests and steep-sided ravines. It is a great climber and often retreats to the safety of a tree if it feels threatened or to rest. Little is known about this secretive cat, but it's thought that it mainly hunts on the ground, where it seeks out small mammals, reptiles and insects.

CAT STATS
Scientific name: *Leopardus guigna* **Habitat:** Moist temperate forests or dense scrubland in central and southern Chile and along the Chile-Argentina border **Weight:** 2.1–3 kg (4.6–6.6 lbs) **Length:** 37–51 cm (14–20 in) plus a 20-25-cm (8–10-in) tail **Conservation status:** Vulnerable

CAT CULTURE

As one of our closest and most captivating animal friends, it's no surprise that cats have slunk into stories and meowed their way into myths for thousands of years. But people's beliefs about what cats' looks and behaviours mean can be very different depending on where in the world they live.

DARK MAGIC

First, let's tackle the biggest cat myth of all – that black cats bring bad luck. This belief was widespread during the Middle Ages in Europe when cats, especially black ones, were associated with witchcraft and cruelly persecuted. Sadly, negative attitudes towards black cats continue to this day. In some parts of America and Europe, black cats in rehoming centres wait much longer than other cats to find their fur-ever homes.

Fortunately, in other parts of the world, black cats are celebrated. In Japan, if you greet a black cat, you will be blessed with good luck. In some English counties, black cats were traditionally given to brides on their wedding day to bring happiness to a marriage. Wherever you live, embrace the paw-sitive and show those beautiful black cats some love.

If you're out after dark in the Scottish Highlands, beware the cat-sith (you say it 'cat-shee'). Said to lurk around graveyards, stealing the souls of the dead, the cat-sith is particularly active on the night of Samhain, the Celtic form of Halloween.

GOOD OMENS

Many cultures of the world hold cats of all colours in high regard – none more than Islam. Viewed as holy animals, cats are cherished in Islamic culture, admired for their cleanliness and given free rein of homes and mosques.

In rural Thailand, cats play an important role in traditional rain ceremonies. Because many cats dislike water, they are associated in Thai culture with dry weather. To welcome the rainy season and bless the rice harvest, a cat was traditionally taken from house to house and had water sprinkled on it. Nowadays, a stuffed toy cat is used, so no kitty needs to get his or her paws wet.

Legend tells how Islam's Prophet Muhammad's cat once fell asleep on his robe. Rather than wake his pet, the Prophet cut his sleeve off, so his cat could snooze in peace.

LAP OF THE GODS

According to Norse myth, Freyja – the goddess of war, death and love – was a massive cat fan. She travelled in a chariot pulled by two giant grey cats. Modern versions of Norse myths often depict Freyja's felines as Norwegian forest cats (p49).

The Maya of Mexico and Central America worshipped various gods and goddesses who took the form of jaguars, including Ix Chel, the goddess of midwifery and medicine, and the sinister 'jaguar god of the underworld', who shifted between worlds of sunlight and shadow.

SHIPS' CATS

Cats have been sailing the world with humans since ancient Egyptian times and have inspired many seafaring superstitions. A black cat on board a ship was traditionally considered lucky by British and Irish sailors, while Japanese seamen thought tortoiseshell cats offered protection against storms.

Seafarers around the world believed cats could predict the weather – and this is true! A cat's heightened senses allow it to detect changes in atmospheric pressure, so it can take cover when it feels wild weather brewing.

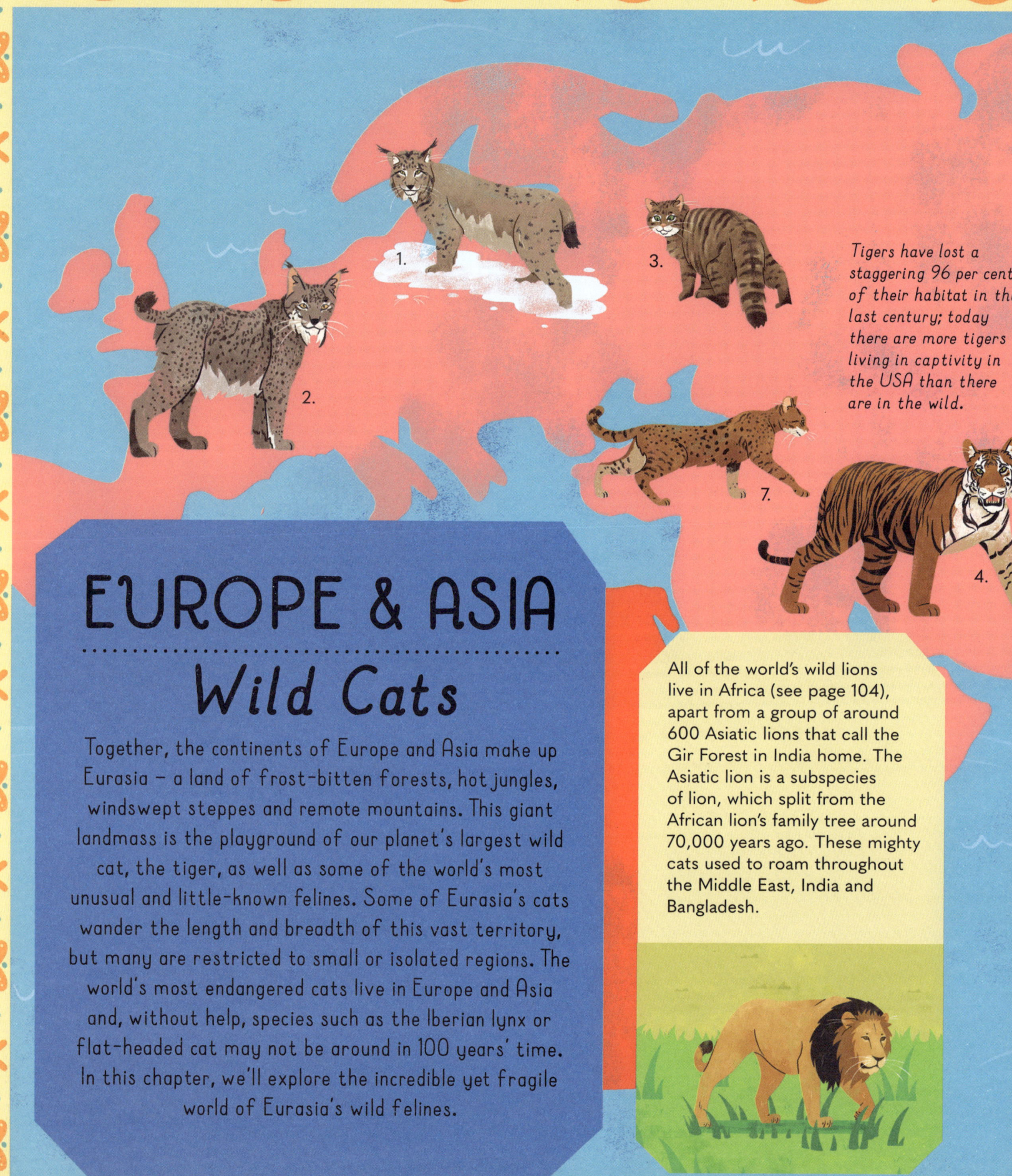

Tigers have lost a staggering 96 per cent of their habitat in the last century; today there are more tigers living in captivity in the USA than there are in the wild.

EUROPE & ASIA
Wild Cats

Together, the continents of Europe and Asia make up Eurasia — a land of frost-bitten forests, hot jungles, windswept steppes and remote mountains. This giant landmass is the playground of our planet's largest wild cat, the tiger, as well as some of the world's most unusual and little-known felines. Some of Eurasia's cats wander the length and breadth of this vast territory, but many are restricted to small or isolated regions. The world's most endangered cats live in Europe and Asia and, without help, species such as the Iberian lynx or flat-headed cat may not be around in 100 years' time. In this chapter, we'll explore the incredible yet fragile world of Eurasia's wild felines.

All of the world's wild lions live in Africa (see page 104), apart from a group of around 600 Asiatic lions that call the Gir Forest in India home. The Asiatic lion is a subspecies of lion, which split from the African lion's family tree around 70,000 years ago. These mighty cats used to roam throughout the Middle East, India and Bangladesh.

Today, there are only around 4,000 snow leopards left in the wild due to poaching and habitat destruction.

1. EURASIAN LYNX
2. IBERIAN LYNX
3. EUROPEAN WILDCAT
4. TIGER
5. SNOW LEOPARD
6. PALLAS'S CAT
7. ASIATIC WILDCAT
8. CHINESE MOUNTAIN CAT
9. JUNGLE CAT
10. RUSTY-SPOTTED CAT
11. FISHING CAT
12. LEOPARD CAT
13. FLAT-HEADED CAT
14. ASIATIC GOLDEN CAT
15. BAY CAT
16. CLOUDED LEOPARD
17. MARBLED CAT

WILD CATS · EUROPE & ASIA

EURASIAN LYNX

In prowls the Eurasian lynx – the largest species of lynx and Europe's third-largest predator. This powerful hunter can be found across Europe and Asia, from dense woodlands in Germany to the rocky slopes of the Himalayas and snowy forests in Siberia. Although it has one of the biggest ranges of any wild cat, it was once even more widespread and has been hunted to extinction in many parts of western Europe.

A Eurasian lynx is about as big as a Labrador dog and can take down prey four times its size. They are especially fond of deer, but will also eat hares, rabbits, mice, foxes and birds. They rest in thickets or caves in the day and mainly hunt at dawn, dusk or night, silently stalking their prey before pouncing.

- Large tufted ears
- Ruff of hair around face
- Grey-brown fur with spots and sometimes small stripes
- Short tail with a black tip
- Wide, furry feet for walking on snow
- Back legs longer than front legs

CAT STATS
Scientific name: *Lynx lynx* **Habitat:** Boreal and deciduous forests, scrub, semi deserts and tundra in Europe, Russia and Central Asia **Weight:** 15–30 kg (33–66 lbs) **Length:** 80–110 cm (31–43 in) plus a 16–23-cm (6–9-in) tail **Conservation status:** Least concern

IBERIAN LYNX

While the Eurasian lynx is one of the world's most widespread cats, the Iberian lynx is one of the world's most threatened. About half the size of its Eurasian cousin, the Iberian lynx is only found in southwest Spain and southern Portugal, where this tufty-eared cat prowls through oak forests and thick scrubland.

By 2002, the number of Iberian lynx left in the wild had shrunk to less than 100, due to habitat loss, illegal hunting and shortages of the lynx's favourite food – rabbits. Today, thanks to conservation efforts, there are around 1,100 Iberian lynx. Like all lynx, Iberian lynx are solitary creatures.

- Short, dark-tipped tail
- Pale-yellow to reddish-brown coat with dark spots
- Pointed ears with large tufts
- Long legs
- Small face with a large beard, which is more distinctive than on other lynx species

CAT STATS
Scientific name: *Lynx pardinus* **Habitat:** Oak forests with dense undergrowth and scrub in Portugal and Spain **Weight:** 7–10 kg (15–22 lbs) **Length:** 68–82 cm (27–32 in) plus a 12.5–15-cm (5–6-in) tail **Conservation status:** Endangered

EUROPEAN WILDCAT

Europe's smallest wild feline, the European wildcat is about the same size as a domestic tabby. These plucky cats live in dense forest habitats, but you'll be lucky to catch sight of one. Stealthy and secretive, European wildcats are most active at dawn and dusk, and generally avoid places where there's lots of human activity.

European wildcats will happily shimmy up trees, but they tend to use their climbing skills to keep themselves out of danger rather than to hunt. If they feel threatened, they'll quickly dart up a tree, or sometimes use a tree to hide food for later (a behaviour known as 'caching'). Wildcats normally hunt on the ground, using their sharp hearing, eyesight and super-sensitive whiskers to search out rabbits and rodents.

How can you tell you're looking at a wildcat rather than a well-fed tabby? Wildcats are generally more muscly than your average household moggie, have longer legs, a large, flat head, and a thick tail that ends in a round dark-coloured tip. They also don't have white tummies or feet, as domestic tabbies often do.

Wildcats can breed with domestic cats. This is one of the greatest threats to wildcat populations, as it means the wildcat's genes and characteristics gradually become weaker and will eventually be lost.

Ears that stick out to the side

Dense tabby-patterned coat, which gets thicker in the winter

Broad head

Some wildcats have a white spot on their throat

Bushy tail with ring pattern and a black tip

CAT STATS

Scientific name: *Felis silvestris* **Habitat:** Mainly dense forest habitat, but has been found living in scrub, grasslands and marshes in continental Europe, Scotland, Sicily, Turkey and the Caucasus Mountains **Weight:** 3–8 kg (7–18 lbs) **Length:** 45–80 cm (18–31 in) plus a 26–33-cm (10–13-in) tail **Conservation status:** Least concern

WILD CATS • EUROPE & ASIA

TIGER

Meet the king of all cats – the tiger, the largest feline in the world. There are six subspecies of tiger alive today: the Siberian (or Amur), South China, Sumatran, Indochinese, Malayan and Bengal.

These unmistakable animals are the only big cat with stripes – and no two tigers have the same pattern. Although the striking orange-and-black combination stands out to us, tigers mainly prey on hoofed animals, such as deer and wild boar, which can't see bright colours. To a deer, it is hard to pick out a tiger hidden among long grass ... until it's too late! When a tiger is close enough, this stealthy hunter will pounce and normally take down its prey with a single, killer bite to the neck.

These magnificent creatures are critically endangered due to habitat loss and poaching. They have lost a staggering 96 per cent of their habitat in the last century.

An adult male Siberian tiger is the largest cat in the world and weighs the same as you and seven of your classmates combined!

Tigers are fond of water and will often take a soak in a river or lake to cool down in hot weather.

- Large, powerful body
- Orange fur with dark-brown or black stripes
- Soft toepads, which help the cat walk silently through the forest
- Excellent eyesight – a tiger's night vision is six times as powerful as a person's, so they hunt well in the dark
- Ruff of hair around face

CAT STATS

Scientific name: *Panthera tigris* **Habitat:** Taiga forest (Siberian tiger only), temperate and tropical forests, grassland, scrub, marshes and mangroves in Asia **Weight:** 75–325 kg (165–717 lbs) **Length:** 146–290 cm (57–114 in) plus a 72–109-cm (28–43-in) tail **Conservation status:** Endangered

Tigers have white spots on the back of their ears. It's thought these markings could be to confuse prey, who might mistake the spots for eyes, or as a way for tiger cubs to keep track of their mum when they're following her through long grass.

A snow leopard uses its thick tail to help it balance and to provide extra warmth when it sleeps. It also uses it to store fat, so it has a back-up energy supply when food is scarce.

Coat is covered in rosette markings and small spots

Large head with green-grey or blue eyes

Long, thick tail

Thick, plush grey fur on body with paler fur on tummy helps the cat blend in with its surroundings

Broad paws act as snowshoes, allowing the cat to move easily over frozen ground

SNOW LEOPARD

Nicknamed the 'ghost of the mountains', the snow leopard is one of the world's most superbly camouflaged cats. It could be staring you in the face from a snowy Himalayan mountainside and you wouldn't spot it.

Secretive and solitary, a snow leopard lives alone for most of its life, roaming isolated peaks in search of wild sheep and ibex. The cat's enormous feet are covered in thick fur, which muffles the sound of its approach, allowing the leopard to creep up on prey unawares before pouncing. These talented cats are also able to spring up to 15 metres (49 feet) horizontally and 6 metres (20 feet) vertically!

CAT STATS
Scientific name: *Panthera uncia* **Habitat:** Alpine meadows, high mountains, rocky areas and glaciers in Central Asia **Weight:** 22–52 kg (49–115 lbs) **Length:** 86–125 cm (34–49 in) plus an 80–105-cm (31–41-in) tail **Conservation status:** Vulnerable

PALLAS'S CAT

This stout cat makes its home in remote grassland (known as a 'steppe') in Central Asia. The Pallas's cat is well adapted to this cold and inhospitable environment, with big paws for clambering over rocks, dense fur for warmth and a bushy tail that it can wrap around itself to keep extra cosy.

Like all cats, the Pallas's cat has thick, see-through third eyelids (called 'nictitating membranes'). These are especially helpful to the Pallas's cat, protecting its eyes from dust and icy winds. The Pallas's cat relies a lot on sight to hunt, seeking out small ground-dwelling animals such as gerbils, voles and pika scuttling about on the windswept plains. When it's not hunting, this secretive feline can be found curled up in caves, crevices or in other animals' disused burrows.

CAT STATS
Scientific name: *Otocolobus manul* **Habitat:** Dry grasslands in Central Asia, especially Mongolia and Russia **Weight:** 2.5–4.5 kg (5.5–10 lbs) **Length:** 46–65 cm (18–25.5 in) plus a 20–31-cm (8–12-in) tail **Conservation status:** Least concern

Flat head and short ears help the cat keep a low profile in open terrain

Big, owl-like eyes with circular pupils

Very thick, grey fur

Black spots on forehead and stripes on tail

Stocky legs with large paws

WILD CATS · EUROPE & ASIA

ASIATIC WILDCAT

Sometimes known as the Asian steppe cat or Indian desert cat, this little wildcat makes its home in rocky crevices or burrows dug by other animals. While Asiatic wildcats prefer to live near water, they can survive in waterless deserts by relying on their prey for moisture – their favourite snacks include grasshoppers, gerbils and lizards. Some have been observed killing king cobras!

CAT STATS
Scientific name: *Felis lybica ornata* **Habitat:** Mountains, deserts and scrub in Kazakhstan, Pakistan, western India, western China and Mongolia **Weight:** 2–6 kg (4.4–13 lbs) **Length:** 47–74 cm (19–29 in) plus a 21–36-cm (8–14-in) tail **Conservation status:** Least concern

JUNGLE CAT

Don't go looking for this long-legged feline in a jungle! It prefers to prowl among reeds and grasses in swamps and wetlands. Home to all sorts of small rodents, fish and birds, these habitats make excellent hunting grounds. Jungle cats are widespread across Asia. A small population has also existed along the River Nile in Africa for thousands of years – the mummified remains of jungle cats have even been found in ancient Egyptian tombs, suggesting they may have been tamed and kept as pets.

CHINESE MOUNTAIN CAT

The Chinese mountain cat is so secretive that it wasn't photographed in the wild until 2007. Found only in China, this chunky cat makes its home in high-altitude rocky grasslands, where it has to cope with both very hot summers and bitterly cold winters. It is known locally as a 'grass cat' because its grey-brown fur allows the cat to blend in perfectly against the dry grass as it hunts rodents, rabbits and pikas (small burrowing animals, related to rabbits).

CAT STATS
Scientific name: *Felis bieti* **Habitat:** Steppe grasslands, alpine meadows, shrubland in China **Weight:** 6.5–9 kg (14–20 lbs) **Length:** 70–84 cm (27–33 in) plus a 32–35-cm (12.5–14-in) tail **Conservation status:** Vulnerable

CAT STATS
Scientific name: *Felis chaus* **Habitat:** Prefer wetlands but also found in grasslands, scrub and forests in Africa, the Middle East, India, southern Asia, tropical China and Southeast Asia **Weight:** 5–9 kg (11–20 lbs) **Length:** 58–76 cm (23–30 in) plus a 21–27-cm (8–11-in) tail **Conservation status:** Least concern

RUSTY-SPOTTED CAT

This fairy-like feline weighs less than an egg when it's born and grows to about half the size of a domestic cat as an adult. Despite being one of the world's tiniest kitties, the rusty-spotted cat is a fierce night-time hunter. Small rodents and insects form the bulk of a rusty cat's diet, but these plucky cats have been known to tackle much bigger prey, such as chickens.

> **CAT STATS**
> **Scientific name:** *Prionailurus rubiginosus* **Habitat:** Forest, grassland, scrub and rocky slopes in India, Sri Lanka and Nepal **Weight:** 1–1.6 kg (2.2–3.5 lbs) **Length:** 35–48 cm (14–19 in) plus a 15–30-cm (6–12-in) tail
> **Conservation status:** Near threatened

LEOPARD CAT

Of all the small wild cats in Asia, the leopard cat is the most widespread. The secret to its success is its adaptability. As well as being comfortable in a range of habitats, including human-made ones such as farmland and plantations, leopard cats hunt in trees and on the ground, are active at night and during the day, and eat a wide range of small prey. One of the most unusual places this cat has been recorded living is a vast network of natural cave systems in Borneo, where it hunts swifts.

FISHING CAT

As its name suggests, this water-loving feline spends most of its time swimming for its supper. With long whiskers to detect movement in the water, powerful legs and partially webbed feet, it is perfectly adapted to hunt fish, frogs and shellfish. It also has a special double coat, with an under layer of very short, dense hair that lies close to the cat's skin so water can't get through it – a bit like a furry wetsuit.

> **CAT STATS**
> **Scientific name:** *Prionailurus viverrinus* **Habitat:** Various water habitats, including marsh, mangrove swamps, streams and rivers in India, Sri Lanka and Southeast Asia **Weight:** 5–16 kg (11–35 lbs) **Length:** 65–86 cm (26–34 in) plus a 25–30-cm (10–12-in) tail **Conservation status:** Vulnerable

> **CAT STATS**
> **Scientific name:** *Prionailurus bengalensis* **Habitat:** Forest, jungle, scrub and semi-desert in India, Pakistan, Afghanistan, Himalayan foothills, China, Russia, most of Southeast Asia, Japan and the Philippines **Weight:** 1.7–7 kg (4–15 lbs) **Length:** 45–75 cm (18–30 in) plus a 19–31-cm (7–12-in) tail
> **Conservation status:** Least concern

WILD CATS • EUROPE & ASIA

FLAT-HEADED CAT

This strange-looking feline spends most of its time in and around water so it can catch its favourite food – fish. It is perfectly adapted to life in a wetland environment, with webbed paws for swimming and wading through muddy ground, and especially sharp teeth for gripping on to slippery prey. This cat's eyes are very close together, which improves its ability to judge distances. Its large eyes also help the cat see well at night, when it is most active.

CAT STATS
Scientific name: *Prionailurus planiceps* **Habitat:** Rainforests, swamps, marshes, lakes, streams and wetlands in Sumatra, Borneo and on the Malayan Peninsula **Weight:** 1.5–2.5 kg (3.3–5.5 lbs) **Length:** 45–52 cm (18–20 in) plus a 12–17-cm (5–7-in) tail **Conservation status:** Endangered

ASIATIC GOLDEN CAT

Although it's called a golden cat, this beautiful feline comes in a kaleidoscope of colours, from fox red and brown to grey and black. Its rich coat is coupled with a striking mask of white and brown stripes on the cat's face, which helps this secretive cat to melt into its forest habitat. Asiatic golden cats are normally active at dawn, dusk or during the night, when they prowl the jungle in search of muntjac and young sambar deer.

CAT STATS
Scientific name: *Catopuma temminckii* **Habitat:** Tropical and sub-tropical evergreen forests in Nepal, northeast India, China, Thailand, Malaysia and Sumatra **Weight:** 8.5–15 kg (19–33 lbs) **Length:** 66–105 cm (26–41 in) plus a 42–57-cm (17–22-in) tail **Conservation status:** Near threatened

BAY CAT

The mysterious bay cat lives on the island of Borneo. Between 1874 and 2003, only 13 bay cats were closely observed, making this feline one of the least-studied wild cats in the world. With chestnut-red fur and striped markings on its face, it looks similar to the larger Asiatic golden cat (see above) but it is actually a separate species. Because it relies on having a thick forest habitat, this beautiful cat is severely threatened by deforestation.

CAT STATS
Scientific name: *Catopuma badia* **Habitat:** Tropical forest on Borneo **Weight:** 3–4 kg (7–9 lbs) **Length:** 53–70 cm (21–28 in) plus a 39-cm (15-in) tail **Conservation status:** Endangered

Because of the way its neck bones are structured, the clouded leopard can't roar like a big cat or purr like a small one. Instead, it communicates with growls, hisses and chuff noises.

CLOUDED LEOPARD

Named after the unique cloud-like markings on its coat, this striking cat spends much of its time resting and hunting in treetops. Despite being a medium-sized cat, the clouded leopard is surprisingly nimble, with large paws to help keep its footing on branches, a long tail for balance, strong back legs for jumping and flexible ankles that allow it to shimmy down trunks headfirst. In proportion to its body size, its upper canine teeth are bigger than any other cat's – possibly to help the leopard keep hold of prey, such as gibbons and macaques, that it catches in the canopy.

A separate species called the Sunda clouded leopard (Neofelis diardi) lives only on the islands of Borneo and Sumatra. Sunda clouded leopards normally have darker fur than mainland clouded leopards, with delicate spots inside their cloud markings.

CAT STATS
Scientific name: *Neofelis nebulosa* **Habitat:** Mainly tropical rainforest in Southeast Asia and China
Weight: 11–23 kg (24–51 lbs) **Length:** 68–106 cm (27–42 in) plus a 61–84-cm (24–33-in) tail
Conservation status: Vulnerable

MARBLED CAT

The marbled cat looks very much like a clouded leopard (see above) in miniature. The size of a house cat, with blotchy markings and large canine teeth, it loves to climb – one was recorded resting 25 metres (82 feet) up a tree in a forest in Borneo. It uses its long, thick tail – which can be longer than the cat's body and head combined – to balance as it climbs and has a habit of scampering down trees headfirst.

CAT STATS
Scientific name: *Pardofelis marmorata* **Habitat:** Tropical forest in Southeast Asia, from south of the Himalayan foothills to Malaysia, Borneo and Sumatra
Weight: 2–5 kg (4–11 lbs) **Length:** 45–62 cm (18–24 in) plus a 35–55-cm (14–22-in) tail **Conservation status:** Near threatened

CHEETAH

BLACK-FOOTED CAT

Cheetahs can't roar. They communicate with one another through a range of growls, purrs and bird-like cheeps!

In proportion to their body, servals have the longest legs of any cat in the world. A serval can leap over 2.5 metres (8.2 feet) high to pluck a low-flying bird from the air!

AFRICA
Wild Cats

Africa is a land of lush savanna grasslands, dense rainforests and the planet's largest hot desert, the Sahara. This unique and beautiful continent is the kingdom of three iconic cat species — the mighty lion, the stealthy leopard and the lightning-quick cheetah. It's also home to six equally fascinating small wild cats. These include the sand cat, a feline that thinks nothing of battling venomous vipers; the black-footed cat, which is so small it makes its home in termite mounds; and the caracal, which can swipe birds from the air in a single leap.

WILD CATS • AFRICA

AFRICAN LION

With its magnificent mane and golden coat, the African lion is one of the most recognisable animals in the world. Its mighty roar can be heard up to 8 kilometres (5 miles) away and once echoed throughout Africa. However, in the last 20 years the number of lions has fallen by about 30 per cent, due to a combination of poaching and habitat loss.

Lions are powerful and fierce but they are also family creatures. They are the only cat that lives in groups, called prides, which are usually made up of around 12 adult females, their cubs and one or two adult males. Males patrol the pride's territory and chase off intruders, while females care for the cubs and work together to catch food.

Lions usually hunt at night so they can sneak up on their prey. Their favourite targets are zebra, wildebeest and antelope, but they will scoff whatever meat they find, including other animals' leftovers. Second to eating, a lion's favourite thing is sleeping – adults snooze for 16–20 hours a day!

CAT STATS
Scientific name: *Panthera leo* **Habitat:** Range of habitats, including scrub, desert, grassy plains (savanna) and woodland in sub-Saharan Africa
Weight: 100–272 kg (243–600 lbs) **Length:** 137–250 cm (53–98 in) plus a 60–100-cm (24–39-in) tail **Conservation status:** Vulnerable

Black tassel at the tip of tail

Long, muscular body

Large head

Lions roar as a team. Every member of the pride, from the biggest male to the littlest cub, gets involved in a roaring session to let other prides know to keep their paws off their territory.

Four large canine teeth for ripping and tearing meat

Males have thick mane around head and shoulders

Large, sharp claws for gripping prey

Only male lions have manes. Their manes grow longer and darker as the lion gets older. As well as looking impressive to females and intimidating to other males, a lion's mane also protects its head and neck during fights.

- Light, tawny-yellow fur with dark, circular spots, known as rosettes
- Spotty markings help camouflage the leopard in treetops or long grass
- Big eyes to help them see in the dark
- Long tail helps the leopard balance when climbing
- Lots of long whiskers
- Strong claws which it uses to grasp prey and climb trees

LEOPARD

If the lion is king of the savanna, the leopard is queen of the treetops. These nimble cats spend much of their time in trees, snoozing on a branch during the day and climbing down at night to hunt antelopes, pigs and deer. They even use trees to store their leftovers, often hauling prey twice their weight into the canopy to keep it safe from hyenas and lions wanting to snatch it for themselves. As well as being expert climbers, leopards are also great swimmers.

Female leopards usually give birth to two cubs at a time. Young leopards stay with their mum for at least 18 months, so they can perfect their hunting and climbing skills.

CAT STATS
Scientific name: *Panthera pardus* **Habitat:** Includes forests, deserts, savanna, mountains in Africa and Asia **Weight:** 37–90 kg (82–200 lbs) **Length:** 90–191 cm (36–75 in) plus a 51–101-cm (20–40-in) tail **Conservation status:** Vulnerable

- Long tail to help balance when running and make quick turns
- Long, flexible spine allows it to take big strides when it runs
- Black 'tear' stripes on face
- Pale-yellow coat with black spots helps it blend into the grass when stalking prey
- Narrow, nimble paws
- Thin, strong legs
- Internal organs are all large to help the cat cope with intense bursts of speed
- Unlike all other cats, the cheetah has claws that can only be partly retracted (pulled back). These give it extra grip while running.

CHEETAH

The cheetah is the Olympic sprinter of the cat world. It is the fastest land animal on the planet, capable of reaching speeds of 96 km (60 miles) per hour in 3 seconds – in other words, a cheetah can accelerate quicker than a racing car! Although they're fast, they can't maintain their top speed for more than 30 seconds, so they must get as close as possible to their prey before pouncing. Cheetahs are most active during the day because they rely on their eyesight for hunting. They chase down small animals they spot, such as birds and rabbits, as well as larger prey like antelope and warthogs.

CAT STATS
Scientific name: *Acinonyx jubatus* **Habitat:** Desert, grasslands and scrub in southern and eastern Africa **Weight:** 21–65 kg (46–143 lbs) **Length:** 113–140 cm (44–55 in) plus a 60–84-cm (24–33-in) tail **Conservation status:** Vulnerable

WILD CATS • AFRICA

SAND CAT

It may look like a kitten lost in the Sahara but don't let the sand cat's cute face fool you – as the only feline that lives exclusively in deserts, this is one tough kitty. The sand cat is mostly active at night, when temperatures are cooler, and shelters underground during the day to escape the desert Sun. It is an excellent digger, using its shovelling skills to build burrows and find prey (with the help of those massive ears). Although it usually hunts rodents, birds and insects, this feisty feline will also attack and eat deadly snakes.

CAT STATS
Scientific name: *Felis margarita* **Habitat:** Sandy and stony deserts in Africa and Asia **Weight:** 1.3–3.4 kg (3–7.5 lbs) **Length:** 39–52 cm (15–20 in) plus a 23–31-cm (9–12-in) tail **Conservation status:** Least concern

SERVAL

This strange-looking cat struts its stuff in savanna and wetlands, using its stilt-like legs and long neck to peer over tall grasses in search of prey and its massive ears to listen out for squeaks and scuttles. Once a serval has found a target, it pounces with pinpoint precision. It catches over 50 per cent of its intended prey – compare that to a whole pride of lions, which have a 30 per cent success rate.

CAT STATS
Scientific name: *Leptailurus serval* **Habitat:** Savanna, wetlands and reedbeds in Africa **Weight:** 7–13.5 kg (15–30 lbs) **Length:** 59–92 cm (23–36 in) plus a 20–38-cm (8–15-in) tail **Conservation status:** Least concern

AFRICAN WILDCAT

It's thought that around 10,000 years ago, a group of these cats were tamed by people and became the ancestors of today's domestic cats. A modern-day African wildcat looks very similar to a pet cat with two exceptions – African wildcats have a rusty-brown tint to the back of their ears and much longer legs. These legs give the cats a distinctly wild way of walking, as they prowl through deserts and scrub on the lookout for mice, rats and voles.

CAT STATS
Scientific name: *Felis lybica* **Habitat:** Various, including deserts, savanna, scrubland, forests and rocky areas in Africa and parts of southwest and Central Asia **Weight:** 3–8 kg (6–18 lbs) **Length:** 45–80 cm (17–31 in) plus a 24–36-cm (9–14-in) tail **Conservation status:** Least concern

CARACAL

Don't mess with a caracal! Thanks to the stiff layer of fur that covers its feet, this stealthy cat barely makes a sound as it slinks towards an unsuspecting bird. If the bird gets startled and takes flight, the hunt is not over. A caracal can leap an incredible 3 metres (9.8 feet) in the air to grab its prey. Along with ninja-like jumping powers, the caracal's distinguishing features are its large, black-tufted ears. Each ear has over 20 muscles (you only have six in yours!), allowing the cat to move them in different directions to detect a meal.

> **CAT STATS**
> **Scientific name:** *Caracal caracal* **Habitat:** Dry savanna, scrubland, woodland and deserts in Africa and Asia **Weight:** 6–20 kg (13–44 lbs) **Length:** 61–105 cm (24–41 in) plus a 19–34-cm (7–13-in) tail **Conservation status:** Least concern

BLACK-FOOTED CAT

Meet Africa's smallest wild cat! According to local legends, this teeny cat can bring down a giraffe. In reality, the largest prey it can tackle successfully is a hare, but it lives up to its fierce reputation, catching between 10 and 14 items of prey each night. By day, it hides in abandoned burrows or old termite mounds and emerges at night to hunt. Despite its name, only the pads of its paws are black. They are also covered in hair to protect the cat's feet as it tiptoes across hot sand.

> **CAT STATS**
> **Scientific name:** *Felis nigripes* **Habitat:** Grassy plains and desert in Botswana, Namibia and South Africa **Weight:** 1–2.5 kg (2.2–5.5 lbs) **Length:** 36–52 cm (14–20 in) plus a 12–20-cm (5–8-in) tail **Conservation status:** Vulnerable

AFRICAN GOLDEN CAT

This so-called golden cat actually comes in two colours – reddish-gold and grey. About twice the size of a pet cat, with a sturdy body and stocky legs, this elusive creature is thought to spend most of its time on the forest floor, stalking rodents, birds and monkeys. It will use the paths carved by forest elephants to navigate its way through the jungle and is rarely seen by humans. Because they depend so much on forests, these cats are severely affected by deforestation, as well as poaching.

> **CAT STATS**
> **Scientific name:** *Caracal aurata* **Habitat:** Tropical forests in west-central Africa and on the west coast **Weight:** 6–14 kg (13–31 lbs) **Length:** 62–94 cm (24–37 in) plus a 25–37-cm (10–15-in) tail **Conservation status:** Vulnerable

RECORD-BREAKING CATS!

£1.50

Cats don't need to be told they're awesome – they already know it. But do you know just how incredible cats are? Read on to learn some fabulous facts about our feline friends.

PURR POWER

Two kitties, Smokey and Merlin, share the record for the loudest purr by a domestic cat. They were each recorded purring at 67.8 decibels. That's about as loud as a washing machine!

Cats purr by vibrating muscles in their vocal cords. The average cat's purr hits a soothing 25 decibels.

TOE-TALLY INCREDIBLE

Cats normally have 18 toes, with five toes on each front paw and four toes on each back paw. A ginger cat called Jake from Ontario, Canada, smashed the record for 'cat with most toes' with a claw-some 28! Cats with more toes than usual are called polydactyl. Polydactyl kitties were popular ships' cats because their extra toes meant they were exceptionally good at climbing the rigging.

ANYTHING IS PAW-SIBLE!

In 2021, a tortoiseshell kitty called Alexis, from Austria, smashed the world record for 'most tricks performed by a cat in a minute'. Some of the 26 tricks Alexis performed included rolling out a red carpet, ringing a bell and crossing her paws.

Buy 30, Get 2 FREE CANS!

WONDERFUL WHISKERS

A Maine coon from Finland called Missi holds the record for the longest whisker on a cat. Missi's super-sized whisker measured 19 cm (7.5 in) – that's longer than a pencil!

Cats usually have around 24 whiskers on their face. They use their whiskers to navigate the world around them and judge how far away things are from their face.

THE DAILY MEOW

The everyday paper for your litter

LARGEST LITTER

The world's largest litter of kittens was born to a Siamese-Burmese cross in the UK in 1970. The cat, called Tarawood Antigone, gave birth to 19 kittens! On average, cats normally have between four and six kittens in a litter.

FELINE FORTUNE

According to Guinness World Records, the title of 'world's wealthiest cat' belongs to a black cat called Blackie from Buckinghamshire, UK. When Blackie's millionaire owner died in 1988, he left £7 million ($12.5 million) to his beloved moggie – today, that sum would be worth around £23 million ($29 million). The funds were split between three cat charities on the condition that they would look after Blackie for the rest of his life.

MR MOUSE TOYS

Catnip down to our **SQUEAK OF THE WEEK SALE!**

REALLY BIG CATS

The largest wild cat is the tiger, but the largest cat in the world is the liger – a cross between a lion and a tiger. Lions and tigers don't mate with each other in the wild, so ligers only exist in captivity. While tigers may weigh up to around 325 kg (717 lbs), the biggest liger recorded weighed a staggering 418.2 kg (922 lbs)!

LITTLE AND LARGE

The smallest cat on record was a male Persian named Tinker Toy. This teeny-weeny cat was only 7 cm (2.75 in) tall and 19 cm (7.5 in) long when fully grown. At the other end of the kitty scale, the longest domestic cat ever was a mighty Maine coon named Stewie. Stewie measured 123 cm (48.5 in) long. That's about half as long as a bed!

GLOSSARY
FOR MORE FUR-RELATED WORDS SEE PAGE 15.

ambush To sneak up on something unawares from a hidden position. Many cats are 'ambush predators', meaning they lie in wait before pouncing on their prey.

blue A light- to dark-grey colour of fur. Breeds such as the British shorthair or Chartreux typically have coats of this colour.

bobtail A cat that is born with a naturally short tail or without a tail.

breed A group of domestic cats that have been bred by humans to have particular characteristics or features.

breeding programme The planned breeding of a group of animals. In the case of domestic cats, breeding programmes can help establish breeds that share similar characteristics or features. In conservation, a breeding programme can help improve the populations of endangered animals.

camouflage An animal's ability to hide itself and blend in with its surroundings. Many wild cats have coat patterns that help them camouflage.

cat fancier A person who breeds and looks after cats.

conservation Taking action to protect and preserve wildlife and the environment.

conservation status A measure of how endangered an animal species is.

crossbreed A domestic cat whose parents are two different breeds.

cub A young wild cat.

deforestation When forests are cut down and not replanted.

Dickin Medal A British medal awarded to an animal that has performed a great act of heroism.

domestication The process of taming a wild animal.

domestic cat Any member of the species *Felis catus*. Also known as house cats and typically kept as pets.

double coat A coat formed of two layers – a rough, weather-resistant topcoat and a soft, thick undercoat.

endangered An animal that is at risk of disappearing forever from the wild.

extinct An animal species that has died out and no longer exists.

fawn A soft light-brown colour of fur.

feline Any member of the cat (or Felidae) family, including pet cats and wild cats. The feline family is split into two main groups – big cats (Pantherinae) and small cats (Felinae).

feral cat A domestic cat that chooses to live a wild life and has little or no contact with humans.

habitat The natural home of an animal (or plant).

habitat loss When a natural habitat is destroyed or reduced, meaning that animals and plants that used to live there struggle to survive.

instinct The natural behaviour of an animal.

kitten A baby cat under 12 months of age.

lilac A light pink-grey colour of fur.

litter A group of kittens born to a mother cat at the same time.

mackerel A tabby cat that has a pattern of thin, curving stripes running across its coat. The stripes resemble a mackerel fish's skeleton.

mammal A warm-blooded animal with a backbone and hair. Mammals feed their young with milk. Cats and humans are examples of mammals.

melanistic An animal that has dark-coloured fur.

moggie A domestic cat that is descended from multiple breeds and crossbreeds.

mouser A cat that is especially skilled at catching mice.

neutering When an animal's reproductive organs are removed by a vet so it cannot have baby animals. This is an important way to keep pet populations under control.

nocturnal An animal that is active at night and asleep during the day.

paw pad One of the tough, thick patches of skin on the bottom of a cat's foot. The paw pad protects the cat's foot.

pedigree A domestic cat descended from cats who have all belonged to the same, particular breed.

poaching The illegal hunting and catching of wild animals.

polydactyl cat A cat that has one or more extra toes.

predator An animal that hunts other animals for food.

prey An animal that is killed by another for food.

retractable claws Claws that can be pulled back into an animal's toe when they are not being used. All cats are able to retract their claws apart from the cheetah.

rex cat Any of several breeds of cat that have dense wavy or curly coats.

ruff Long, thick hair that grows around the neck.

savanna A flat area of grassland, with few trees, usually found in tropical parts of the world.

seal A dark-brown colour of fur. Certain breeds, such as the Siamese, typically have 'seal point' coats, meaning they have a cream-coloured body and dark-brown paws, nose, ears and tail (or 'points').

selective breeding The process in which people deliberately breed animals so they have particular qualities. These can be practical skills, behavioural traits or physical features. The breeds of cat featured in this book are the result of years of selective breeding.

species A group of living things that have similar characteristics and can breed with each other.

stalk To follow prey quietly and stealthily.

steppe A large, flat area of dry grassland, typically found in eastern Europe and Central Asia.

stray cat A domestic cat that is friendly with humans but has left or lost its home.

tufts A cluster of hairs, typically growing between a cat's toes or on the tips of its ears.

undercoat Soft, thick fur that sits underneath a longer and typically rougher topcoat.

webbed feet Feet that have a piece of skin between the toes. Having webbed feet can help animals to swim in water.

whiskers Long, sensitive hairs that grow on the faces of many animals, including cats.

whisker pad The area on the side of a cat's face where whiskers grow.

INDEX

Abyssinians 20, 32, 33, 60, 64, 66, 70, 73, 76
Afghanistan 40, 99
Africa 20, 37, 43, 50–51, 60, 70, 79, 92, 98, 102–107
African golden cats 102, 107
African wildcats 12, 60, 102, 106
agouti 15, 46, 70, 76
Alice's Adventures in Wonderland 38
American bobtails 8, 16, 21
American curls 9, 16, 29
American shorthairs 16, 25, 27, 28, 29, 33, 41, 42, 74
American wirehairs 16, 29
ancient Aztecs 18
ancient Egypt 12, 18, 50, 52–53
ancient Egyptians 12, 50, 52–53, 70, 91, 98
ancient Maya 91
ancient Romans 38, 48
Andean cats 82, 83, 88
Andes Mountains, the 88, 89
Aphrodites 36, 47
Arabian maus 54, 61
Argentina 83, 88, 89
Asia 12, 19, 46, 55, 56–61, 64–71, 79, 88, 92, 94, 96–101, 105, 106, 107
Asian group (domestic cats) 74–75
  Asian smoke 75
  Asian tabby 74
  Bombay 74
  Burmilla 75
  Tiffanie (or Burmilla longhair) 75
Asiatic golden cats 93, 100
Asiatic lions 92
Asiatic wildcats 93, 98
Australasia 65, 76–77
Australia 6, 12, 13, 64, 65, 76
Australian mists 13, 64, 76
Austria 108

Balinese 16, 25
Bangladesh 92
Bastet (ancient Egyptian goddess) 52–53
bay cats 93, 100
Bengals (domestic breed) 12, 16, 17, 32, 33, 60
big cats 6, 78, 82, 96, 101, 103, 109
Birmans 36, 37, 46, 77
black cats 90, 91, 109
black-footed cats 103, 107
bobcats 21, 83, 84
bobtailed domestic breeds 8, 16, 19, 21, 41, 55, 57, 64, 67, 70
body language 62–63
Bolivia 83, 88
Borneo 99, 100, 101
Botswana 107
Brazil 88, 89
breed (definition of) 13
British longhairs 36, 39
British shorthairs 28, 36, 38, 39, 41, 42, 48
Burmese 19, 25, 32, 64, 65, 66, 71, 74, 75, 76, 77, 109

camouflage 8, 51, 84, 85, 87, 88, 97, 105
Canada 16, 18–19, 83, 84, 108

Canada lynx 78, 82, 83, 84
caracal 6, 78, 102–103, 107
cat agility (courses and competitions) 27, 33, 35, 73
cat cafes 65
cat fanciers 34, 35
cat shows 34–35
catamount 85
Caucasus Mountains, the 95
Central America 85, 86, 87, 91
Central Asia 60, 94, 97, 102, 106
Ceylon (domestic breed) 64, 71
Chartreux 13, 36, 37, 47
cheetahs 9, 78, 88, 103, 105
Cheshire Cat, the 38
Chile 83, 88, 89
China 22, 64, 66, 70, 98, 99, 100, 101, 102
Chinese mountain cats 93, 98
claws 9, 34, 43, 49, 81, 105
clouded leopards 6, 78, 93, 101
Cornish rex 15, 36, 42, 48
Costa Rica 89
cougars 85
cubs 85, 96, 104, 105
Cymrics 16, 19
Cyprus 36, 37, 47

deforestation 86, 100, 107
Devon rex 36, 42
Dickin Medal, the 22
dogs 20, 22, 23, 27, 31, 42, 81, 94
domestic cats (*Felis catus*) 6–7, 8–9, 12–77, 78, 80–81, 89, 95, 99, 106, 108–109
domestication (process of) 12, 52, 106
Donskoys 54, 56
double coats 8, 14, 19, 40, 41, 49, 56, 57, 99

Egypt (modern country – see also ancient Egypt) 36, 47, 50
Egyptian maus 32, 36, 50
endangered cats 7, 79, 88, 92, 94, 96, 100
Ethiopia 70
Eurasian lynx 93, 94
Europe 12, 36–43, 46–49, 56, 59, 69, 79, 90, 92, 94–95
European shorthairs 36, 48
European wildcats 93, 95
exotic shorthairs 15, 16, 17, 25

farm cats 13, 24, 29, 30, 41, 48, 49
Felidae 6
Felinae 6, 78
feral cats 6, 7, 21, 30, 51, 61
Finland 48, 108
fishing cats 93, 99
flat-headed cats 92, 93, 100
France 23, 36, 46, 47
Freyja (Norse goddess) 91

Geoffroy's cats 83, 88
German rex 36, 48
Germany 36, 48, 94

habitat loss 94, 96, 102, 104
Hagia Sophia 54
hairless breeds 15, 18, 30, 56
Havana (domestic breed) 43
Hermitage museum 55
heroic cats 22–23

Himalayas, the 94, 97, 99, 101
hybrid cats 32

Iberian lynx 79, 92, 93, 94
India 74, 79, 92, 98, 99, 100, 102
indoor cats 13, 32, 49, 56, 76
Iran 40, 47
Islamic culture and cats 91
Isle of Man 41
Israel and the Palestinian Territories 47, 54, 60
Italy 38, 71
IUCN Red List of Threatened Species 7
Ix Chel (Maya goddess) 91

jaguars 6, 78, 82, 83, 85, 86, 91
jaguarundis 83, 88
Japan 57, 64, 65, 67, 90, 99
Japanese bobtails 64, 67
jungle cats 93, 98

Kanaani 54, 60
Kazakhstan 98
Kenya 13, 36, 51
khao manees 64, 68
kittens 7, 13, 18, 20, 21, 25, 27, 29, 39, 41, 42, 43, 44–45, 48, 51, 56, 63, 66, 73, 75, 76, 77, 87, 106, 109
kodkods 83, 89
korats 64, 68
Kuril Islands, the 57
Kurilian bobtails 55, 57
Kuwait 61

LaPerms 16, 30
Lake Van 58
leopards 6, 74, 78, 86, 102, 103, 105
leopard cats 32, 93, 99
li huas 64, 66
ligers 109
lions 6, 17, 52, 78, 79, 85, 92, 102, 103, 104, 105, 109
longhaired domestic cats 8, 14, 19, 20, 21, 23, 25, 24, 26, 27, 29, 30, 31, 34, 39, 41, 58, 59, 67, 70, 73, 75
lykois 16, 30

Maine coons 13, 16, 17, 24, 108, 109
Malaysia 100, 101
Mandalays 64, 77
Manx 8, 19, 36, 41
marbled cats 93, 101
margays 78, 82, 83, 87
Mekong bobtails 64, 70
Mekong River, the 70
Mexico 84, 91
mice 12, 13, 24, 28, 53, 55, 66, 87, 89, 94, 106
microchipping 44
Middle East, the 61, 92, 98
minuets 16, 31
moggies 12, 13, 14, 17, 27, 28, 34, 48, 54, 64, 77, 95, 109
Mongolia 97, 98
mountain lions 85
munchkins 16, 31
Myanmar 46, 64, 71, 77

Namibia 107
natural instincts 7, 32, 80–81

Nepal 99, 100
neutering 45
New Zealand 64, 65, 77
North America 16–21, 24–33, 79, 82–85
northern tiger cats 83, 89
Norway 36, 49
Norwegian forest cats 36, 49, 91

ocelots 6, 33, 78, 82, 83, 87
ocicats 16, 33
Oriental group (domestic cats) 72–73
  Foreign white 72
  Oriental longhair 73
  Oriental shaded 73
  Oriental shorthairs 60
  Oriental tabby 73
  Oriental tortoiseshell 72

Pakistan 98, 99
Pallas's cats 93, 97
Pampas cats 83, 89
Pantherinae 6, 78
Paraguay 88, 89
Persians 14, 15, 20, 25, 27, 31, 35, 36, 39, 40, 41, 43, 59, 73, 75, 109
Peru 83, 88
Philippines 99
pixiebobs 16, 21
poaching 93, 96, 102, 104, 107
polydactyl cats 21, 108
Portugal 79, 94
pumas 6, 78, 82, 83, 85, 88

Qatar 61

ragamuffins 16, 27
ragdolls 12, 14, 16, 26, 27
rats 22, 24, 28, 53, 55, 106
record-breaking cats 108–109
rescue and rehoming centres 13, 20, 90
River Nile, the 98
Russia 23, 54, 55, 56–57, 94, 97, 99
Russian blues 42, 54, 56
rusty-spotted cats 78, 93, 99

Sahara Desert, the 103, 106
sand cats 78, 102, 103, 106
Saudi Arabia 61
Scandinavia 49
Scotland 41, 95
Scottish folds 9, 36, 41
Scottish straights 41
Sekhmet (ancient Egyptian goddess) 52
Selkirk rex 16, 20
senses 10–11, 91
servals 6, 78, 102, 106
Seychelles, the 43
Seychellois 36, 43
ships' cats 22, 28, 41, 49, 56, 91, 108
shorthaired domestic cats 8, 14, 15, 16, 17, 19, 20, 21, 25, 27, 28, 29, 32, 33, 34, 36, 38, 39, 41, 42, 47, 48, 50, 51, 54, 55, 56, 57, 59, 60, 61, 66, 67, 68, 69, 70, 71, 72, 73, 74, 75, 76, 77
short-legged cat breeds 31
Siamese 6, 13, 19, 25, 27, 33, 42, 43, 64, 65, 69, 70, 72, 73, 109

Siberia 57, 94
Siberians (domestic breed) 6, 14, 55, 57
Singapore 64, 66
Singapuras 64, 66
small wild cats 78, 84, 88–89, 94–95, 97, 98–100, 101, 103, 106–107
snow leopards 6, 78, 93, 97
snowshoes (domestic breed) 16, 27
Sokokes 13, 36, 51
Somalis (domestic breed) 16, 20, 70
South Africa 107
South America 79, 82–83, 85, 86–89
Southeast Asia 46, 64, 65, 66, 70, 98, 99, 101
southern Asia 65, 98
southern tiger cats 83, 89
Spain 79, 94
sphynxes 12, 15, 16, 17, 18
Sri Lanka 64, 71, 99
stray cats 6, 21, 22, 29, 42, 48, 56
Suffolk (domestic cat breed) 36, 43
Sumatra 100, 101
Sunda clouded leopard 6, 101
Sweden 36, 48

tabbies 15, 18, 19, 21, 23, 24, 25, 27, 28, 30, 31, 32, 33, 38, 39, 40, 41, 42, 43, 46, 47, 48, 49, 51, 57, 59, 60, 61, 66, 69, 71, 72, 73, 74, 76, 89, 95
teeth 9, 44, 82 86, 100, 101, 104
templecats 64, 77
Thailand 64, 68–69, 70, 72, 91, 100
The Aristocats 54
tigers 6, 33, 78, 79, 85, 92, 93, 96, 109
tongues 9
Tonkinese 16, 19
tortoiseshells 15, 18, 19, 20, 21, 25, 26, 27, 30, 31, 38, 39, 40, 41, 42, 43, 46, 47, 48, 49, 57, 59, 67, 69, 71, 72, 91, 108
toygers 16, 33
Turkey 47, 49, 54, 58–59, 95
Turkish Angoras 39, 54, 59
Turkish shorthairs 54, 59
Turkish Vans 54, 58

UK 26, 36, 38–43, 49, 70, 71, 72, 74, 75, 109
United Arab Emirates 54, 61
Uruguay 88
USA 16, 19–21, 20–21, 23, 24–33, 35, 67, 68, 71, 74, 92

vaccinations 44
Vankedisis 58
Vikings 49

Wales 19
whiskers 9, 11, 18, 20, 29, 42, 48, 56, 95, 99, 105, 108
wild cats 6–7, 8, 15, 21, 32, 33, 66, 78–79, 81, 82–89, 92–107
World War II 48, 55

Yangtze River, the 22